SRI LANකA™

Paradise Isle Publications
London

www.elitesrilanka.com

2nd Edition

ISBN 978-0-9534963-7-2

Art & Design by Eshan Goonesekera

Cover design San Kara

In the beginning
God created the Heavens
and the Earth...

When Adam descended
from Heaven,
he left his footprint
on a mountain
as he set foot
in the
Garden of Eden...
Sri Lanka

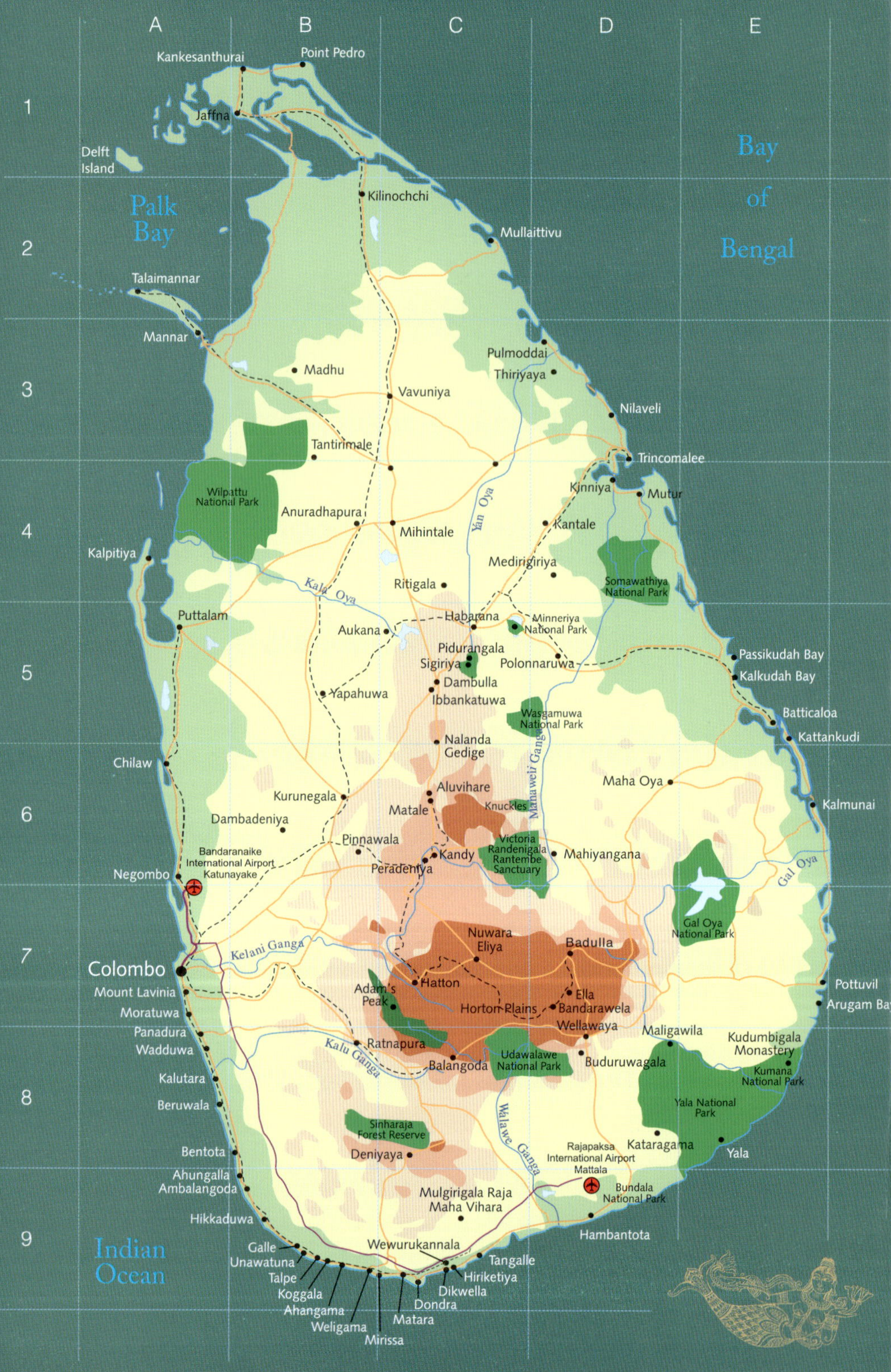

A
B
C
D
E
1
2
3
4
5
6
7
8
9
Kankesanthurai
Point Pedro
Jaffna
Delft Island
Palk Bay
Bay of Bengal
Kilinochchi
Mullaittivu
Talaimannar
Mannar
Madhu
Pulmoddai
Thiriyaya
Vavuniya
Nilaveli
Tantirimale
Trincomalee
Wilpattu National Park
Kinniya
Mutur
Anuradhapura
Mihintale
Yan Oya
Kantale
Kalpitiya
Medirigiriya
Somawathiya National Park
Ritigala
Kala Oya
Puttalam
Habarana
Minneriya National Park
Aukana
Pidurangala
Sigiriya
Polonnaruwa
Passikudah Bay
Kalkudah Bay
Dambulla
Yapahuwa
Ibbankatuwa
Wasgamuwa National Park
Batticaloa
Kattankudi
Nalanda Gedige
Chilaw
Mahaweli Ganga
Maha Oya
Aluvihare
Kurunegala
Kalmunai
Matale
Knuckles
Dambadeniya
Pinnawala
Victoria Randenigala Rantembe Sanctuary
Kandy
Mahiyangana
Bandaranaike International Airport Katunayake
Negombo
Peradeniya
Gal Oya
Gal Oya National Park
Nuwara Eliya
Badulla
Kelani Ganga
Colombo
Hatton
Mount Lavinia
Adam's Peak
Ella
Pottuvil
Moratuwa
Horton Plains
Bandarawela
Arugam Bay
Panadura
Wellawaya
Maligawila
Kudumbigala Monastery
Wadduwa
Ratnapura
Kalu Ganga
Buduruwagala
Balangoda
Udawalawe National Park
Kumana National Park
Kalutara
Beruwala
Yala National Park
Sinharaja Forest Reserve
Walawe Ganga
Rajapaksa International Airport Mattala
Kataragama
Yala
Bentota
Deniyaya
Ahungalla
Ambalangoda
Bundala National Park
Mulgirigala Raja Maha Vihara
Hikkaduwa
Hambantota
Indian Ocean
Galle
Wewurukannala
Unawatuna
Tangalle
Talpe
Hiriketiya
Koggala
Dikwella
Ahangama
Dondra
Weligama
Matara
Mirissa

Index

Contents

The Sinhalese සිහලුන්

Prince Vijaya was the legendary forefather of the Sinhalese. He was the eldest son of eight sets of twins born to King Sinhabahu and Queen Sinhasivali. Sinhabahu was the eldest son born of the union of a beautiful Indian princess and a lion ("Sinha" in Sanskrit).

With the blessings of Lord Buddha and with 700 followers, Vijaya set sail from his kingdom in northern India to the ancient land of Lanka. He landed on the north-west coast of the island on the very day that Lord Buddha passed away into Nirvana in 483 BC. Vijaya named the island "Tambapanni", meaning copper-coloured, after the coppery sands of the shore. This land was destined to be the home of Buddhism.

On this island lived two tribes the "Yakkhas" and "Nagas". Princess Kuveni of the Yakkha tribe set about seducing Vijaya and in return she gave him her kingdom. Thus Prince Vijaya became King, and the lion race, the "Sinhalese", was born.

Lion Race

Enchanting People

අසිරිමත් ජනතාව

From the very first travellers that visited the little island to modern-day tourists, their first impressions have been similar - they are universally captivated by the enchanting smile of the island's inhabitants.

Sri Lanka has a rich ethnic diversity with a racial and cultural mix of Sinhalese, Tamils, Muslims, Burghers, and Veddhas. Over the years these cultures have blended uniquely, creating the charm and charisma that is quintessentially Sri Lanka.

Smiling

For many thousands of years, the island was inhabited by the Yakkhas and Nagas; Stone Age hunter-gatherers who had originally walked to the island from the tip of India when the two were joined together. The Veddhas are descendants of these tribes and have more racial affinities with Australian Aborigines than with any of the island's other Aryan and Dravidian colonisers. The Veddha population is ever diminishing due to marriage outside their communities, the loss of forests to the expanding population, and urbanisation. Sadly, the island's oldest culture is now on the brink of extinction as only a few hundred Veddhas remain.

The dominant ethnic group on the island are the Sinhalese, who trace their ancestry to Vijaya, the Northern Indian Prince who arrived on the island in the 5th Century BC. The Sinhalese have developed a unique cultural identity with Buddhism as a central aspect. Around 74 per cent of the island's population is Sinhalese, the majority of whom are Buddhist.

The Tamils are the second largest ethnic group on the island, making up 18 per cent of the population. The Tamils are themselves divided into two main groups. The Sri Lankan Tamils (12.5 per cent) were the descendants of the Southern Indian Pandyan and Chola Kingdoms who invaded the island from the 2nd Century BC. The second group are the Indian Tamils (5.5 per cent) who are the descendants of the South Indian labourers brought to the island by the British in the 19th Century to work on the newly established coffee and then tea plantations. The majority of Tamils are Hindu - around 20 per cent are Christian.

As Sri Lanka is strategically positioned at the crossroads of major sailing routes, it inevitably attracted several other ethnic groups who were destined to make Sri Lanka their home. Arab seafarers first visited the island centuries before Christ. From around the 9th Century, these Muslim traders (known as Moors) established trading settlements on the west coast of the island. They were joined by the Malays who descended from the regiments brought over by the Dutch. The Bohras and Memons were enlisted from India by the British.

The Burghers are the descendants of intermarriages between European settlers and the local population. They usually speak English as their mother tongue. The word "Burgher" is Dutch for citizen and was used to describe descendants of the Dutch colonists who came to work for the Dutch East India Company. Over time, the term Burgher has also come to include Sri Lankans who are descendants of the Portuguese and British.

Collectively, around 70 per cent of Sri Lankans are Buddhists, 15 per cent are Hindu, 7.5 per cent are Muslim and 7.5 per cent are Christian.

COLOMBO

N 06° 56′ 04″
E 79° 50′ 41″

Colombo began as a small seaport visited by Arab, Persian and Chinese traders. The name Colombo may have derived from the Sinhala word "kolamba", which means port or harbour.

Between the 9th and 16th centuries, this small port town was predominantly populated by Muslims of Arab descent. In the early 16th century the Portuguese arrived and built a fort in Colombo, but when the Dutch captured the city in 1656, the Portuguese occupation came to an end.

The British invaded Colombo in 1798 and, after the capturing of Kandy in 1815, Colombo became the capital of Ceylon as the island was then called. The British ruled Ceylon until its independence on 4th February 1948.

Kolamba

The Dutch destroyed most signs of Portuguese presence when they besieged and bombarded Colombo in order to drive them out. The Dutch rebuilt the fort to protect their trade in cinnamon, sapphires, ivory and elephants and also introduced town planning.

However it was the British who made the most drastic changes to the landscape. They tore down the defences and transformed the city into a thriving international port. They were also responsible for the construction of roads, railways and administrative buildings. Although the fortification was demolished, the area where it was located came to be known as "Fort".

Today, a stroll around the Fort area reveals remnants of colonial rule, with some Dutch architecture mixed in with British constructions and modern buildings.

Adjoining Fort is Pettah, an extensive, lively, colourful market bazaar. Created in the 16th century for the merchants, it sells everything that the locals could possibly want to buy. It is a great place to wander around and the Dutch museum at 95 Prince Street is well worth a visit. Colombo's main railway station, Fort, and the bus station are adjacent to Pettah.

The Grand Oriental

Formerly the Taprobane, the Grand Oriental Hotel or GOH was founded in 1837. Situated at 2 York Street, Fort, and located opposite the harbour, it was the "in place" to be seen during the colonial era. The fourth floor Harbour Room Restaurant serves a decent buffet lunch with an unrivalled view of Colombo harbour.

The Colombo National Museum is housed in an impressive classical colonial building established in 1877 by a former British Governor and positioned in the heart of Colombo close to the Town Hall. The museum contains pre and early historical relics with a collection of treasures from Anuradhapura, Polonnaruwa and Kandy. Exhibits include Buddhist and Hindu bronzes, stone statues, frescoes, antique furniture, and an array of royal regalia belonging to the Kings of Kandy.

For art lovers, Colombo's art galleries show off a diversity of artistic talent. The Colombo Art Gallery features major exhibitions of accomplished painters and photographers. The Sapumal Foundation has a superb collection of works by the acclaimed '43 group of Sri Lankan artists. Galleries like the Lionel Wendt often exhibit both traditional and modern works while Barefoot Art Gallery and Paradise Road Gallery Café regularly showcase works by contemporary masters.

Colombo has several performing art centres including the Lionel Wendt, the Elphinstone, the Tower Hall and the Navarangahala, all popular venues for musical performances and theatrical productions. The Nelum Pokuna or "Lotus Pond" is Colombo's newest performing arts theatre which is the largest in Southeast Asia. It includes a state-of-the-art auditorium that can seat an audience of over 1200 as well as an open-air amphitheatre.

The island is adorned with Buddhist shrines, Hindu Kovils, Islamic Mosques and Christian churches. It is not unusual to see a religious edifice of one faith next to the holy site of another.

Gangarama Temple

Situated opposite the Beira Lake is the delightful Gangarama Temple. It is a very well known place of worship and quite unique, complete with a Dagoba, Bo Tree, image house, relic chamber containing relics of the Buddha, museum, library, and at one time, its most revered cohabitant - their very own temple elephant. Unusually it also possesses a collection of vintage cars and printing presses.

During the Full Moon or "Poya" day in February, the Temple hosts a most colourful festival called the Navam Perahera, a spectacular pageant of thousands of traditional dancers and drummers accompanied by hundreds of caparisoned elephants.

Saint Anthony's Church, Kochchikade

Saint Anthony's Shrine, located in Kochchikade, Colombo, is a Roman Catholic Church dedicated to Saint Anthony of Padua and is designated a National Shrine and Minor Basilica.

In the early 18th century, during Dutch rule, a time when practising the Catholic Religion was banned, an Indian priest and missionary by the name of Father Joseph Vaz (1651-1711) came to evangelise on the island, accompanied by Father Antonio from Cochin. Father Antonio, who was assigned to Colombo began evangelising to the local fisherfolk. As his popularity grew, he built a chapel made of mud on the seashore to honour Saint Anthony of Padua, his patron saint. When Father Antonio passed away, as per his wish, he was buried in the chapel.

Later in 1806, the chapel was enlarged and in 1822, a member of the congregation brought a statue of St. Anthony from Goa which was placed upon the altar of the church. In 1828, construction of a new church in the neo-classical style commenced and was consecrated in 1834.

The statue to this day is held in great veneration and attracts devotees of all faiths as it is widely acknowledged that St. Anthony's Kochchikade is a place where miracles take place. In 1995 when Pope John Paul II visited Sri Lanka to beatify Ven. Joseph Vaz, he made an unscheduled visit to St. Anthony's, which was in itself considered a minor miracle.

In commemoration of the 175th Jubilee of St. Anthony's Church in 2010, holy relics of St. Anthony of Padua were brought to the island and placed at the shrine for a brief time.

St. Anthony's was sadly targeted in the Easter Sunday Attacks that took place in 2019. Many worshippers lost their lives and the church was badly damaged. It was later restored and today remains a symbol of hope with Sri Lankans united and standing together.

The Church is famous for its Annual Feast of Saint Anthony which attracts many thousands of devotees of all faiths from around the world.

Bellanwilla Raja Maha Viharaya

Located near Dehiwala about 7.5 miles (12 km) south of Colombo city, Bellanwilla Temple is one of the most venerated and sacred shrines on the island.

Ancient texts state that Bellanwilla's Bo Tree is one of the 32 saplings that sprouted from the sacred Bo Tree at Anuradhapura planted in the 3rd century BC.

The temple houses large Buddha statues; reclining, seated, and standing, and has some of the most stunning murals which adorn the temple's walls and ceiling.

The Bellanwilla Esala Perahera is an annual festival that takes place during August or September, drawing devotees from all over the island.

Kelaniya Raja Maha Viharaya

Built on the banks of the Kelaniya River about 7 miles (11 km) from Colombo city is one of the oldest and most sacred Buddhist temples in Sri Lanka.

It is believed that on the invitation of Maniakkhika the Naga King of Kelaniya, eight years after gaining enlightenment in the 5th century BC, Lord Buddha together with 500 Arahats (supremely enlightened beings) visited Kelaniya to preach His Dhamma, the Buddhist doctrine, to the King and inhabitants of the island. This was Lord Buddha's third and final visit to the Island.

Ancient texts record that before preaching, Lord Buddha bathed in the waters of the Kelani River, thus making it sacred to the people of Sri Lanka and to commemorate His visit the king built a dagaba on the hallowed spot where the Buddha preached. Within the dagaba was enshrined the jewel-encrusted throne on which the Buddha sat as He preached.

The Kelaniya Temple's image house contains a large gold-plated reclining Buddha and the temple houses striking paintings depicting important events in the life of the Buddha. The spectacular annual Duruthu Perahera is held every January at Kelaniya Temple.

As part of Sri Lanka's 50th Anniversary of Independence celebrations in February 1998, the Guest of Honour HRH Prince Charles visited Kelaniya Temple and offered flowers to a statue of Lord Buddha.

Vishnu Kovil, Dehiwala

Colombo is an exciting and intriguing city with lots of energy and a distinct cosmopolitan vibe. In addition to parks and gardens, street markets, coffee shops and patisseries, there is a superfluity of shopping on hand from bookshops and gift shops, to mega shopping centres with a wide choice on offer for the bargain hunter as well as the most discerning of shoppers. Everything is available from chic designer fashion essentials to state-of-the-art electronic goods.

If you prefer a more relaxed approach then there is the legendary Royal Colombo Golf Club. With scenic fairways and exclusive tranquil surroundings this legacy of the British is truly an oasis in the city.

Or, for an even more relaxed approach, Colombo boasts excellent aromatherapy and Ayurvedic health spas. Together with yoga and meditation centres these soothing therapies are the perfect remedy to relieve pressures of modern living and to rejuvenate the fatigued traveller.

The constant hustle and bustle and jostling for position amongst the ubiquitous tuk tuks is a constant reminder that Colombo is a metropolitan city and the country's commercial heart.

Sri Lanka is renowned for its precious and semi-precious gemstones including Blue Sapphires, Red Rubies, Cat's Eyes, Alexandrites, Tourmalines, Zircons, Garnets, Amethysts and Topaz. Colombo has the best choice of swish jewellery retail outlets; there is something for every age and pocket. Given a little time jewellers can even create pieces customised to your very own design.

Colombo has a gastronomical assortment of dining experiences from trendy cafés and fast-food outlets to the very finest of restaurants serving food of exceptional quality. Local cuisine is a delicious combination of delicate rice and fragrant curries, String Hoppers - a noodle dish made with rice flour served with a spicy coconut milk gravy, Lamprais – a medley of rice and curries baked in a banana leaf, Kothu Roti - a fusion of diced meat and spicy vegetables sautéed with sliced up Godamba Roti, as well as fiery sambols.

Complemented with live music venues, pubs, clubs and casinos the charming city offers everything that would be expected in a truly modern capital.

Sir Henry Ward constructed the Galle Face Green esplanade on his retirement as Governor to the island in 1859. Stretching between the old Parliament building and the Galle Face Hotel, bordering the Indian Ocean and 1 mile (1.6 km) long, this narrow rectangle of open land was dedicated to the ladies and children of Colombo.

The Old Parliament Building Circa 1910

In its heyday, the Green hosted horse races and sports events. Nowadays, early mornings attract people of all ages to exercise on the Green, from a brisk walk to a power jog. In the afternoons, youngsters play softball cricket, and dusk provides the perfect setting for kite flying. At sunset, the Green serves as a romantic rendezvous for courting couples, customarily occupying one bench per pair and employing open umbrellas for privacy. Late at night, Galle Face Green is alive with vendors of exotic foods for the night's revellers.

Located on the southern end of Galle Face Green is the Galle Face Hotel. Built in 1864 and named after the Green, the grand old colonial hotel is the unique and unmistakable edifice that epitomises Colombo, an aide memoire of its glorious history and heritage, the jewel in the crown of the Empire with quite a reputation for having accommodated an illustrious cast of the rich and famous from around the world. One of the many famous guests that stayed within this magnificent palace was the British playwright Noel Coward. It is believed that this was where he wrote his most famous ditty "Mad dogs and Englishmen", apparently playing his first rendition at the piano in the terrace bar. The hotel hasn't changed much since the lyrics of his tongue-in-cheek lampoon of British colonial mentality resonated around the airy halls, - (and the piano probably hasn't been tuned since either).

Prior to the hotel stood the Galle Face Boarding House. One night during the 1840's lodgers were abruptly awoken and greeted with the sight of an unexploded 30lb cannonball in their midst. It had been accidentally fired through the roof by the British Royal Artillery Company (the Ceylon Gun Lascars). Marking this event, the Galle Face Hotel annually hosts the famous "Cannonball Run".

EMBASSIES
1. Australia E5
2. Canada F5
3. China F5
4. European Community F5
5. France F5
6. Germany D6
7. India B4
8. Italy F6
9. Japan F5
10. Malaysia D5
11. Maldives F7
12 Netherlands F6
13. Norway F5
14. Pakistan F4
15. Russia D5
16. Sweden F5
17. Switzerland G5
18. Thailand C4
19. United Kingdom F5
20. USA C5
INFORMATION & SHOPPING
21. Tourist Board C4
22. Tourist Police B3
23. Central Bank B3
24. Central Bus Stand D3
25. Railway Tours Office C3
26. General Post Office B3
27. Liberty Plaza C5
28. State Pharmacy E4
29. Majestic City D6
30. Crescat Boulevard C5
31. Laksala E6
32. World Trade Centre B2
33. Presidential Secretariat B2
34. Dept. of Archaeology D5
35. One Galle Face Mall B4
36. Havelock City Mall F7
PLACES OF INTEREST
37. Golf Course H5
38. President's Residence B3
39. Prime Minister's Residence C5
40. National Museum E5
41. National Archives E5
42. BMICH F6
43. Art Gallery E5
44. Vihara Maha Devi Park E5
45. Town Hall E5
46. Planetarium E6
47. Nelum Pokuna Theatre E6
48. Independence Memorial F5
BUDDHIST TEMPLES
49. Vajiraramaya D6
50. Deepaduttaramaya E2
A B C D E F G H
1 2 3
Harbour
PORT CITY
Mattakkuliya
Kelani River
Peliyagoda
KANDY ROAD
Muthwal
MADAMPITIYA ROAD
ALUTHMAWATHA ROAD
CYRIL C PERERA MAWATHA
Bloemendhal
Grandpass
NEW KELANI BRIDGE ROAD
Kotahena
JAMPETTAH STREET
GRANDPASS ROAD
DR. DANISTER DE SILVA MAWATHA
Orugodawatta
CENTRAL ROAD
DAM STREET
MAIN STREET
Pettah
MEERANIYA STREET
Maligawatta
Hultsdorf
CHURCH ST
YORK ST
MARINE DRIVE
LOTUS RD
OLCOTT MAWATHA
FORT RAILWAY STATION
Beira Lake
Maradana
Maradana Railway Station
Dematagoda
Premadasa Stadium
Sugathadasa Stadium

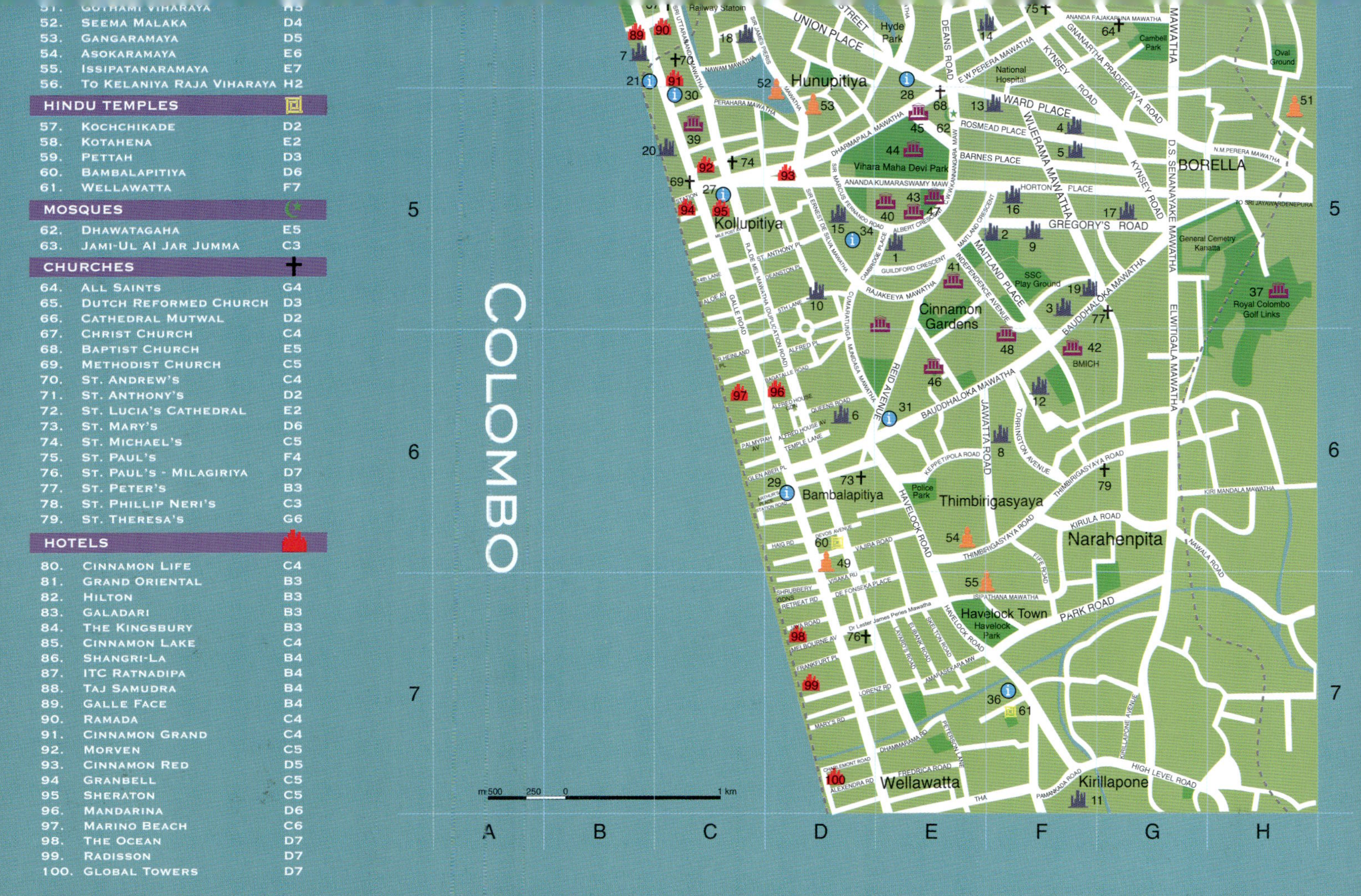
51. Gothami Viharaya H5
52. Seema Malaka D4
53. Gangaramaya D5
54. Asokaramaya E6
55. Issipatanaramaya E7
56. To Kelaniya Raja Viharaya H2
Hindu Temples
57. Kochchikade D2
58. Kotahena E2
59. Pettah D3
60. Bambalapitiya D6
61. Wellawatta F7
Mosques
62. Dhawatagaha E5
63. Jami-Ul Al Jar Jumma C3
Churches
64. All Saints G4
65. Dutch Reformed Church D3
66. Cathedral Mutwal D2
67. Christ Church C4
68. Baptist Church E5
69. Methodist Church C5
70. St. Andrew's C4
71. St. Anthony's D2
72. St. Lucia's Cathedral E2
73. St. Mary's D6
74. St. Michael's C5
75. St. Paul's F4
76. St. Paul's - Milagiriya D7
77. St. Peter's B3
78. St. Phillip Neri's C3
79. St. Theresa's G6
Hotels
80. Cinnamon Life C4
81. Grand Oriental B3
82. Hilton B3
83. Galadari B3
84. The Kingsbury B3
85. Cinnamon Lake C4
86. Shangri-La B4
87. ITC Ratnadipa B4
88. Taj Samudra B4
89. Galle Face B4
90. Ramada C4
91. Cinnamon Grand C4
92. Morven C5
93. Cinnamon Red D5
94 Granbell C5
95 Sheraton C5
96. Mandarina D6
97. Marino Beach C6
98. The Ocean D7
99. Radisson D7
100. Global Towers D7
Colombo
Hunupitiya
Kollupitiya
Cinnamon Gardens
Bambalapitiya
Thimbirigasyaya
Narahenpita
Havelock Town
Wellawatta
Kirillapone
Borella
Vihara Maha Devi Park
Royal Colombo Golf Links
General Cemetry Kanatta
SSC Play Ground
BMICH
National Hospital
Hyde Park
Police Park
Havelock Park
Oval Ground
Cambell Park
Railway Statoin
Union Place
Deans Road
Ward Place
Rosmead Place
Barnes Place
Horton Place
Wijerama Mawatha
Kynsey Road
Gregory's Road
Maitland Place
Independence Avenue
Reid Avenue
Baudhaloka Mawatha
Jawatta Road
Torrington Avenue
Havelock Road
Galle Road
R.A.De Mel Mawatha (Duplication Road)
Park Road
Kirula Road
High Level Road
D.S. Senanayake Mawatha
Elwitigala Mawatha
Gnanartha Pradeepaya Road
Thimbirigasyaya Road
Nawala Road
m 500 250 0 1 km
5
6
7
A B C D E F G H

NEGOMBO

N 07° 12' 37"
E 79° 50' 31"

Only a 15-minute drive from Sri Lanka's Bandaranaike International Airport is the beach resort and colourful fishing village of Negombo.

Located 23 miles (37 km) north of Colombo, Negombo was one of the most important sources of prized cinnamon common to Sri Lanka's southwest coast. Cinnamon was used in medicines and for flavouring foods.

The town grew with the importance of the cinnamon trade in the 17th century. In 1640 the Portuguese constructed a fort here and built churches converting the local Karava fisher folk to Catholicism.

Cinnamon Coast

The Dutch East India Company ousted the Portuguese in 1644, strengthened the fort and built churches for Protestant worship.

To facilitate the transportation of cinnamon (the most profitable spice traded by the Dutch East India Company), spices and gemstones, the Dutch built the canal from Colombo via Negombo to Chilaw and on to Puttalam, a distance of around 80 miles (130 km).

By the time the British arrived in 1796, the demand for cinnamon had decreased, and with the British constructing roads and railways, the canal would become redundant.

Today, Negombo is the country's main fishing port and the centre for prawn and shrimp fishing. Fishermen still use ancient outrigger canoes, or "oruvas", made of jackwood and similar in design to the Arab dhows.

The fish market is open Monday to Saturday and requires an early morning start. Among the exotic specimens on display are catches of seer fish, prawns, crabs and lobsters.

The old Portuguese fort still exists; the British utilised it as a jail, a function for which it is still used today.

Along the beach and due north of the lagoon are Negombo's oceanfront hotels. Negombo's close proximity to the airport provides a convenient resort in which to stay both on arrival before beginning a cultural tour, or as a final night of relaxation before departing from Sri Lanka.

N 07° 18' 03"
E 80° 23' 14"

PINNAWALA ELEPHANT ORPHANAGE

පින්නවල අලි අනාථාගාරය

The Pinnawala Elephant Orphanage was set up in 1975 to provide care for young elephants that had been orphaned due to poaching and would otherwise have faced certain death. Located 50 miles (80 km) from Colombo, Pinnawala is one of Sri Lanka's most popular attractions.

Sri Lankan and other Asian elephants in general, are slightly smaller than their African cousins, and also characterised by smaller ears.

Pinnawala is home to over 85 elephants and a successful breeding programme has led to elephants being born in the orphanage. It is recognised as the world's largest managed group of elephants in human care.

Feeding times are at 9:15am, 1:15pm and 5pm, when the baby elephants are bottle-fed. After the morning and afternoon feeds (between 10am-12pm and 2pm-4pm), the elephants are escorted out of their compound, across the road and down a lane to the nearby river to bathe.

It is quite a spectacle to see these magnificent beasts thunder down the narrow street, only just missing the stalls lined with merchandise displayed to entice the tourists.

It is a good idea to get down to the river before the herd and relax in one of the cafés overlooking the bank while watching the elephants lumber down. For visitors, this twice-daily ritual provides an ideal opportunity to photograph elephants in such a superb setting.

Pinnawala is open 365 days a year and the income generated from entrance fees helps in covering costs for the orphanage's upkeep.

As the orphans are domesticated and accustomed to human care, they cannot be returned to the jungles. When they reach maturity, these animals will join the ranks of working elephants and some will go on to become respected temple elephants.

Life Of The Buddha

බුදුන් වහන්සේගේ ජීවන කතාවස්තුව

Prince Siddhartha Gautama was born on the night of full-moon under a Sala tree in the gardens of Lumbini, at the foothills of the Himalayas, in 563 BC. He was the son of King Suddhodana and Queen Maya and, as a young prince, he led a life of pure luxury. At the age of 16, he married Princess Yasodhara who gave birth to a son called Rahula.

Despite his sumptuous surroundings and his beautiful wife and child, Prince Siddhartha found his carefree, self-indulgent existence wholly unfulfilling. At the age of 29, accompanied by his favourite charioteer, Channa, he visited the more squalid regions of his great city. He saw for himself the reality of poverty, disease, old age and death.

On his return he announced his decision to abandon his home and family. Discarding his princely clothes for the orange robes of a hermit, he opted for a life of asceticism in search of salvation. After six years of being profoundly disillusioned, he meditated for 40 days under the shade of a large Bodhi tree at Bodhgaya in Northern India. Protected by the hood of a giant cobra, he resisted assaults from Mara, the figure in Buddhism who symbolises the forces of delusion, desire, fear, and death, that hinder spiritual progress, and on the night of full-moon, Prince Siddhartha attained the state of Enlightenment.

Bahirawakanda - Kandy

Buddha, the "Enlightened One", devoted the rest of his life to teaching his doctrines, "Dhamma", in India. He passed away into Nirvana on the night of a full-moon in 483 BC at the age of 80.

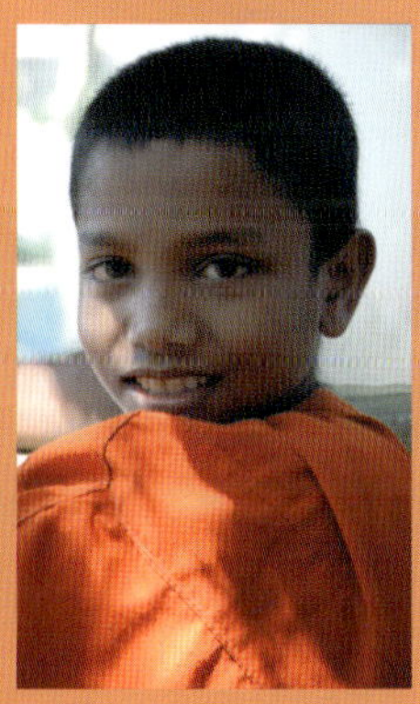

At the core of the Buddha's Enlightenment was the realisation of the Four Noble Truths:

(1) Life is suffering.

(2) The cause of suffering is ignorance and desire.

(3) Suffering can be ended by overcoming desire and attachment.

(4) The path leading to the cessation of suffering is the Noble Eightfold Path. This Path consists of: right views; right intention; right speech; right action; right livelihood; right effort; right-mindedness; and right contemplation. These eight are usually divided into three categories that form the cornerstone of Buddhist faith: morality, wisdom, and samadhi, or concentration.

Salvation lies in achieving Nirvana or freedom from the wheel of rebirth. When Enlightenment is eventually reached by means of the Noble Eightfold Path, the entity is admitted into Nirvana, which is a condition merging the spirit into the infinite good. Nirvana can only be achieved through bodily death. The reward is salvation; the cycle of rebirth ends, and Nirvana, a state of oneness with all, is attained.

The teaching of the Buddha is an invitation to come and see, not to come and believe. The Buddha discovered and showed the Path to Liberation, Nirvana. But we must tread the Path ourselves.

අනුරාධපුර

N 08° 21' 13"
E 80° 24' 06"

ANURADHAPURA

Many centuries before Christ, while the Greek Empire was flourishing in the Mediterranean and other regions were emerging from the late Stone Age, a highly advanced civilisation inhabited the ancient land of Lanka. Cities were orderly, with superb irrigation systems and linked with fine roads.

Anuradhapura became the capital of the island in 380 BC and excavations on the site confirm that human settlement began here about 500 BC. According to the Mahavamsa (the history of the civilisation written by monks in the 5th century AD), the founder of the city was Anuradha, a close follower of Prince Vijaya, the legendary forefather of the Sinhalese race.

Anuradhapura, situated in the North Central province, was a great thriving city and remained the capital for about 1,400 years until the 10th century AD. At the height of its glory the city covered 250 square miles (650 square km) and had a population of tens of thousands.

Elite GUIDE

Ancient Capital

Houses in the city were two and three storeys high, with possibly two levels underground as well. The king lived in a bejewelled palace of 1,000 chambers, with gold-pinnacled shrines that rose hundreds of feet into the air.

The most sacred place in Anuradhapura is the Sri Maha Bodhi (A), the one living relic of past splendour. This huge Bo Tree (*Ficus Religiosa*) was grown from a sapling from the original Bo Tree beneath which the Buddha attained supreme enlightenment in Bodhgaya, India. The sapling was brought to the island by Princess Sanghamitta (sister of Mahinda, who introduced Buddhism to Sri Lanka), on the December full-moon around 240 BC.

The worshipping of the Bo Tree has continued unbroken for 23 centuries. In fact, this is the oldest historically documented human-planted tree on Earth; the original tree in India was destroyed. It is believed that this Bo Tree has been protected and nurtured throughout its history by the descendants of the guardians appointed by King Devanampiya Tissa (250-210 BC) who originally received the sapling.

In the 3rd century BC, King Devanampiya Tissa built the Chapter House as a residence for the monks who were guardians of the tree; this was converted into the Brazen Palace (B), a nine-storey building with 1,000 rooms and a bronze tiled roof, which gave the palace its name. Due to the ravages of time, 1,600 stone columns are all that remains of King Parakramabahu's (1153-1186) final restoration.

The Ruwanweliseya (C), also known as Maha Thupa or "Great Stupa", built in the 2nd century BC, is regarded as the greatest of all the dagobas at Anuradhapura. Guarded by a wall of hundreds of elephants, the Ruwanweliseya was probably the finest construction attributed to King Dutugamunu (161-137 BC), and certainly his last; it was completed as he lay on his deathbed.

Enshrined in the dagoba are various items of immense value, including gems, gold statues and relics of Lord Buddha. Renovations throughout Anuradhapura's history have not been able to attain the full height or the perfect "water bubble" shape of the original building. A statue of Dutugamunu proudly stands facing the great dagoba.

The Mahavamsa and Culavamsa

The Mahavamsa or "Great Dynasty" was the work of Buddhist monks (Bhikkhus) in the 5th century. This Pali chronicle, written on palm-leaf tablets, details the history of the ancient kings and the Buddhist civilisation from the advent of Vijaya in 483 BC to the 4th century AD.

Its continuation, the Culavamsa or "Lesser Dynasty", charts the medieval history of the island up to the arrival of the Portuguese in the 16th century.

Thuparama Dagoba

The Thuparama Dagoba (D) was built by King Devanampiya Tissa (250-210 BC) in 245 BC. This was the first dagoba constructed on the island, and enshrines (amongst other sacred relics) the alms bowl and right collarbone of Lord Buddha, sent by Emperor Asoka after Prince Mahinda's conversion of Anuradhapura. The King built this dagoba in the shape of a "heap of paddy"; its present "bell" shape is the result of restorations. The columns around the Thuparama once supported a building with circular walls and a ring-shaped roof, which enclosed all but the spire.

The giant Jetavanarama Dagoba (E) was built of solid brick in the 3rd century AD by King Mahasena (AD 274-301). It would have originally stood at over 390 ft (120 m) and was the largest dagoba in the world.

The 11th century Palace of Vijayabahu I (F) was hurriedly erected for the coronation of the king in the ancient royal city before he departed to make Polonnaruwa his capital.

Northeast of the palace are the ruins of the Mahapali Refectory (G) or monks' refectory. Here, there is a massive 10 ft (3 m) trough which was filled with rice, donated to the monks, by their followers.

The ancient Temple of the Tooth, Dalada Maligawa (H), distinguished by its tall stone columns, was the first home of the Tooth relic in Sri Lanka when it arrived on the island in AD 331.

Northeast is the unusual Nakha Vihara (I), a square brick dagoba of the later Anuradhapura period.

King Vattagamani Abhaya ascended to the throne in 103 BC, but his reign was shortlived - he was driven out of Anuradhapura by the invading Cholas. In 89 BC, Vattagamani assembled an army, defeated the Cholas and regained his throne. He built the Abhayagiri Dagoba (J) in 88 BC as part of a monastery accommodating 5,000 monks.

Samadhi Buddha

The Kuttam Pokuna (K), or Twin Ponds, are a beautiful pair of 3rd century AD monks' bathing pools. Although called the "Twin Ponds", one is noticeably larger than the other. There were underground ducts bringing water into these ponds and others emptying them.

The Samadhi Buddha (L) dates from the 4th century AD. This superb image is of the serene Buddha seated in a meditative position.

The Ratnaprasada (M) or Gem Palace was built in the 8th century AD. It has two of the best preserved guardstones in Anuradhapura. A guardian spirit, Nagaraja or "Cobra King", holds a vase of plenty and a flowering branch to symbolise prosperity. He is crowned with a cobra hood and at his feet is a dwarf.

Lankarama Dagoba (N) was built in the 1st century BC by King Vattagamani Abhaya as part of a vatadage or circular relic house.

The Mirisaveti Dagoba (O) was built by Dutugamunu between 161 and 158 BC to commemorate his victory over Elara and his assumption of the kingship.

Anuradhapura has three great water tanks. The largest is Nuwara Wewa, 3,000 acres (1,200 hectares), which was created in the 2nd century AD. The oldest tank, dating from the 4th century BC, is Basawakkulama, 300 acres (120 hectares). Tissa Wewa, 400 acres (160 hectares), was built by King Devanampiya Tissa in the 3rd century BC.

The Royal Pleasure Gardens are east of Tissa Wewa tank.

Isurumuniya Temple (P) was built in the 3rd century BC by King Devanampiya Tissa (250-210 BC). This beautiful temple carved out of solid rock had been lost to the jungle until the British rediscovered it in the 1870s. Outside the rocky outcrop is the ceremonial bathing pool. Inside the temple is a large Buddha image, which has been cut from the rock. Stone steps to the side of the temple lead to a dagoba and a great view of the countryside.

The museum at the base of the temple houses Anuradhapura's most famous rock carving, "The Lovers". These figures probably represent Dutugamunu's son Saliya and his low caste lover Asokamala.

In 1982, the sacred city of Anuradhapura was designated a World Heritage Site by UNESCO.

Isurumuniya Temple

The Dagoba

දාගැබ

The dagoba is the most distinctive creation of Buddhist architecture in Sri Lanka. Its origins are probably older than Buddhism and may have derived from the primitive earthen sepulchral mound which developed also into stupas in India, chedis in Thailand and pagodas in China and Japan.

The basic form is the same, built on a raised square terrace, a solid hemispherical brick dome enshrining the relic chamber, crowned with a square block of brickwork containing offerings, adorned with the conical spire. Dagobas are not temples, but monuments built over sacred relics, or constructed to mark a sacred place.

When King Devanampiya Tissa (250-210 BC) received sacred relics including the alms bowl and collar bone of Lord Buddha from Emperor Asoka in India, it was clearly necessary to build an imposing edifice to house them. Thus the first dagoba, the Thuparama, was created in Anuradhapura in 245 BC.

The design of dagobas has symbolic meaning and represents a model of the Buddhist cosmos. The hemisphere is the dome of heaven, the axis of the cosmos represented by the central pinnacle on top. It is customary to walk around dagobas in a clockwise direction following the rotation of the celestial bodies.

There are six different types of dagoba of which the "Bell" is the favourite shape with the designers of these structures. The "Chatty" or Water-pot shape was never popular and has been abandoned, while the "Bubble"shape was fashionable in early times. The "Heap-of-Paddy" is a very ancient form of dagoba and the "lotus", representing the unopened lotus bud, is one of the rarest forms. The "Nelli" dagoba is supposed to represent the form of the fruit of the Nelli tree.

The dagobas vary in size, from miniature votive models to the impressive structure at Anuradhapura, which is larger than all but two of the great Egyptian pyramids.

Thuparama Dagoba

Mihintale

මිහින්තලේ

N 08° 21′ 02″
E 80° 30′ 59″

Mihintale is situated about 10 miles (16 km) east of Anuradhapura. This rocky hill is regarded as the cradle of Buddhism in Sri Lanka. It was here that Prince Mahinda, son of the Indian Emperor Asoka, preached to King Devanampiya Tissa (250-210 BC) during Poson (June full-moon) in 247 BC. King Tissa, whose capital was Anuradhapura, was out hunting and the impromptu meeting resulted in the King, his family and the local inhabitants embracing Buddhism.

Countless pilgrims have since visited Mihintale, "Mahinda's Mountain", to venerate the shrines, dagobas and caves found on the sacred hill.

At the foot of Mihintale are the ruins of an ancient hospital said to be the oldest hospital in the world.

Sacred Rock

The staircase, three flights with 1,840 steps, was built by King Bhatika Abhaya (22 BC-AD 7). At the top of the first flight, a smaller flight to the right leads to a plateau and the Kantaka Cetiya, a 2nd century BC dagoba excavated in 1934. It is 40 ft (12 m) high (originally it would have stood around 100 ft [30 m]), and has four stone flower altars facing the cardinal points.

The second flight of steps continues to a larger plateau. Here are the remains of monastic buildings such as the relic house, two inscribed stone slabs reminding monks of monastic rules, the remains of the Assembly Hall and the Monks' Refectory. The refectory has two huge stone troughs which lay-followers kept filled with rice for the monks.

Karma

Karma keeps account of a person's actions, good or bad, during their life. Human actions lead to rebirth, and the consequences are that whilst good deeds are rewarded, inevitably evil deeds are punished and paid for in the next life.

Karma follows a more natural moral law rather than a system of divine judgment. It determines such issues as one's species, beauty, intelligence, longevity, wealth and social status.

Enlightenment is possible only for humans.

The final stairway leads to the Ambasthala Dagoba, built over the spot where Mahinda appeared to King Devanampiya Tissa. Ambasthala, meaning "mango tree", refers to the subject about which Mahinda quizzed the King to test his intelligence. This dagoba was probably built shortly after the death of King Tissa. Nearby is the Aradhana Gala the "rock of convocation" from which Mahinda first preached.

A path from the Ambasthala Dagoba leads to the summit and the 1st Century BC Mahaseya Dagoba, which enshrines a single hair of Lord Buddha. From here there are excellent views of the Anuradhapura dagobas.

The large boulder to the east is called Mahinda's Bed, where the prince meditated and slept. Another path leads to the Naga Pokuna, "pond of the serpent", a rock pool with a seven-headed cobra hewn from the rock, with its tail reaching the bottom of the pool. This was one of the main sources of water at Mihintale. It was connected by means of channels to the Monk's Refectory and to the Sinha Pokuna, or "Lion Pond", where a carved lion cistern spouted water from its mouth.

N 08° 0' 39"
E 80° 30' 46"

AUKANA BUDDHA

අවුකන පිළිමය

About 30 miles (50 km) south of Mihintale is the Aukana Buddha, one of the most beautiful, perfectly preserved, ancient Buddha images on the island.

This 5th century statue, attributed to King Dhatusena (AD 459-477), is carved out of solid rock and measures 42 ft (13 m) in height.

Aukana means "sun-eating" and the image is best viewed as the sun rises.

Nirvana

The ultimate goal of a Buddhist is freedom from the wheel of continual rebirth with its inherent suffering. This Enlightened state where desire, hatred, and ignorance have been extinguished, is called Nirvana. Nirvana is a state of consciousness merging the spirit into the infinite good, a state of oneness with all.

Nirvana is attainable by anyone. For those unable to pursue the ultimate goal of Nirvana, an objective of better rebirth through improved karma is an option. This is generally practised by lay Buddhists in the hope that it will eventually lead to a life in which they are capable of pursuing final Enlightenment as members of the Sangha, the order of monks.

Elite
GUIDE
Buddha Statues

RITIGALA FOREST MONASTERY

N 08° 07' 04"
E 80° 39' 57"

Located around 25 miles (40 km) southeast of Anuradhapura, rising over 2,000 ft (610 m) above its surroundings, home to an ancient Buddhist monastery, is the Ritigala mountain, dating back to the 1st century BC.

Legend relates that, when flying over the Island, Lord Hanuman, the Monkey God, accidentally dropped a chunk of the Himalayan Mountain he was carrying from India onto Ritigala. The mountain contained rare medicinal herbs and plants that Hanuman needed to save the life of Lord Rama's brother, Prince Lakshman, who was wounded in battle.

The Pali chronicle Mahavamsa states that King Pandukabhaya (437-367 BC), took refuge and established his garrison at Ritigala from where he overthrew his uncles and marched on to establish the Royal city of Anuradhapura.

In the 3rd century BC, after embracing the Buddha Dhamma (Buddhist doctrines), the first ordained Buddhist monk resided here. This serene environment then developed into a monastery for 500 monks to preach and meditate.

Covering an area of 59 acres (24 hectares) the ruins of Ritigala are on the Eastern side of the mountain. At the base of the monastic complex is the Banda Pokuna, a reservoir attributed to King Pandukabhaya, which serves as a ritual bathing tank for those entering the monastery. From here, navigating clockwise, a stone pathway and steps meander upward through the forest across stone bridges linking the ruins of edifices of the monastery. Three large circular platforms placed at intervals serve as resting areas. On one plateau are the ruins of an ayurvedic hospital containing grinding stones to pound the medicinal herbs growing in this unusual microclimate, and a huge stone cut oil bath used for ayurvedic treatments.

Of the rare flora that grows at Ritigala are 337 varieties of trees of which 54 are endemic.

MEDIRIGIRIYA MONASTERY

මැදිරිගිරිය පිරිවෙන

N 08° 09' 22"
E 80° 59' 45"

The first recorded reference of the Medirigiriya Monastery, located in the Polonnaruwa kingdom, was as a place of worship during the reign of King Kanitta (AD 165 - 193). However ancient Brahmi characters engraved on bricks and stone carvings at the site, confirm an earlier history dating from the pre-Christian Era.

The site houses an Image House, bathing ponds, an ayurvedic hospital with a medicine trough for herbal baths and is set upon a rocky outcrop. The masterpiece of the Monastery is the Medirigiriya Vatadage constructed during the reign of King Aggabodhi IV (AD 667 – 683). A Vatadage is a stupa, a circular relic house, encircled by pillars which support a wooden roof. The Medirigiriya Vatadage has three concentric rows of stone pillars surrounded by four large seated Buddha statues facing the cardinal points.

Vatadage

Polonnaruwa

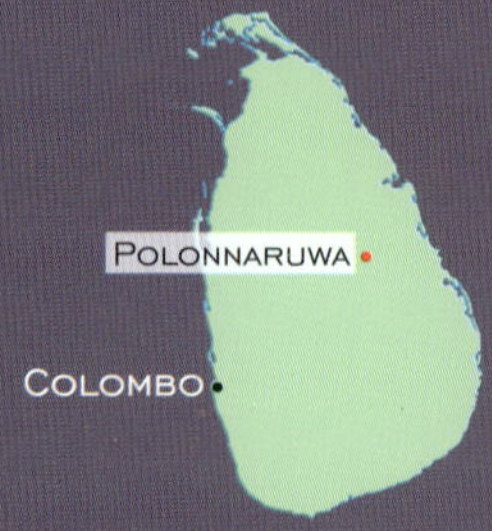

පොළොන්නරුව

N 07° 56′ 38″
E 81° 50′ 01″

After conquering Anuradhapura in the late 10th century, the Cholas decided to move the capital to Polonnaruwa. Inhabited since the 2nd century BC, Polonnaruwa was thought to be better placed strategically to guard against rebellions from the Sinhalese Ruhuna Kingdom in the Southern Province.

In 1073, King Vijayabahu I (1055-1110) drove away the Cholas from the island and restored the Sinhalese throne. He kept Polonnaruwa as the capital, and reconstituted the Buddhist Sangha, the order of monks, which had been demoralised by the Indian occupation. Vijayabahu devoted his reign to rebuilding the country, improving irrigation systems and strengthening the inner core of Buddhism.

Medieval Capital

In the latter part of the 12th century, the work was continued by Parakramabahu I (1153-1186). Under his guidance, huge buildings were erected and, importantly, the Parakrama Samudra (Sea of Parakrama), a 5,900-acre (2,400-hectare) reservoir or "tank", was created. To this day, the tank remains the life-blood of the region.

Parakrama Samudra

Nissanka Malla (1187-1196), in an attempt to surpass his predecessors' achievements, also left very attractive monuments to his name.

The Polonnaruwa Kingdom came to an end in 1215, when the Southern Indians invaded and liquidated the kingdom. Polonnaruwa was left to return to the jungle. From this period onward, the location of the capital city changed several times before finally settling in Kandy in the 16th century.

In the 19th century, the British excavated the site and found it had been previously looted by the Portuguese.

As the island's capital, Polonnaruwa, situated 50 miles (80 km) south-east of Anuradhapura, had a brief history of 200 years and a dozen rulers compared with Anuradhapura's 1,400 years and 123 kings. Unlike Anuradhapura, where the ruins are widely scattered, Polonnaruwa's chief monuments are well preserved and easily accessible. A sensible place to start a tour would be the southern part of the ancient town.

The Pothgul Vihara (1), or "Library Shrine", is a hollow, central, circular brick building surrounded by four small dagobas. This building may have served as a library and, as acoustics are excellent, possibly even used for the chanting of Buddhist texts.

Just north of the shrine is a 12th century statue often called The Sage (2). No one is exactly sure who this 12 ft (3.6 m) high bearded figure represents. However, it is widely believed to be King Parakramabahu I holding an object which represents the "yoke of kingship".

Travelling north and to the east of the Rest House is the entrance to the main site.

Lord Buddha was exceptional in reaching Buddhahood without entering into Nirvana. The Master separated these normally simultaneous spiritual experiences in order for the world to profit from His doctrines.

The Sage

The Royal Citadel was the inner fortress and administrative centre of Parakramabahu's ancient capital. The largest building standing within its clearly visible walls is the impressive Vejayanta Pasada (3), the royal palace of Parakramabahu I. The ruins of three storeys of the original seven remain, with empty sockets in the great brick walls indicating where wooden beams supported higher storeys. Many smaller chambers and the remnants of stairways are evident.

Vejayanta Pasada

Audience Hall

Parakramabahu's Audience Hall (4) is situated directly east of the palace. This great hall, with elegantly carved pillars positioned on a three-tiered stone platform, was apparently connected to the palace by a covered colonnade. Two flights of steps, each with a moonstone, are at the building's entrance. A bas-relief frieze of elephants adorns the base, with every elephant in a different pose. This building was the king's formal centre of government and legislation.

Just below the citadel walls to the east is a large, exquisite, stepped bath of cut stone. The Kumara Pokuna (5), or "royal bath", is of intricate geometrical design. Underground stone conduits feed water from the Parakrama Samudra. The bath would have once been surrounded by a lovely garden of flowering bushes and fruit trees. Immediately next to it is the changing room.

Further north, just below the Quadrangle, is the 13th century Shiva Devale (6) dating from the period when the Southern Indians were briefly in occupation. The stonework is of fine quality and profuse ornamentation so magnificently fitted together as to require no mortar whatsoever. It rivals that of any South Indian shrine of its period. The domed brick roof has collapsed.

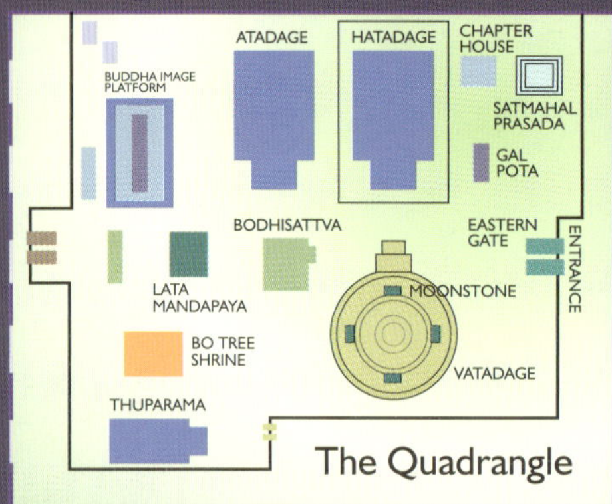

Polonnaruwa's centrepiece, the Terrace of the Tooth Relic, also known as "The Quadrangle", consists of a group of magnificent buildings in a raised area bounded by a wall in the heart of the ancient city.

The Vatadage is the circular building with concentric terraces on your left as you enter. It is probably the oldest monument in Polonnaruwa, several centuries older than the establishment of the city as the capital.

Other vatadages known in Sri Lanka date from around the 7th century and this one has an inscription which attributes it to King Silameghavanna (619-628) of Anuradhapura. The dagoba around which it was constructed was also part of an early monastery. At the entrance to the building, on either side of the moonstone, are a pair of guardstones preventing evil from entering.

Vatadage

The Naga King with a seven headed cobra hood holds a flower-filled pot-of-plenty in one hand and a blossom-laden branch of prosperity in the other. Two dwarf attendants are at the King's feet. In the centre of the Vatadage, within the concentric stone columns that once supported a conical roof, four Buddha statues face the cardinal points, their backs to the sacred mound of brick – all that remains of the dagoba.

Directly opposite the Vatadage is the Hatadage, a Temple of the Tooth attributed to Nissanka Malla (1187-1196). Solid stone walls surround the lower storey, while the upper storey of wood, where the Tooth Relic would have resided, has long since disintegrated. The walls of the building are inscribed with accounts of Nissanka Malla's deeds.

To the west of the Hatadage is the Atadage. Built in the 11th century by Vijayabahu I (1055-1110), this was the original Temple of the Tooth in Polonnaruwa. The decorated ornamental pillars of the ground floor once supported the upper storey where the Tooth relic and other treasures would have been kept. Atadage means "House of Eight Relics".

On the north-western corner of the quadrangle is a platform that once housed a Reclining Buddha Image. A long brick outline is all that remains.

To the south is the late 12th century Lata Mandapaya, a beautiful pavilion with curving vine-like pillars representing lotus stems. This was King Nissanka Malla's "flower scroll hall" where he listened to chanted Buddhist texts.

Lata Mandapaya

The image of the Bodhisattva or "Enlightened being" stands in the centre of the terrace to remind onlookers of the ideal towards which the good Buddhist should aspire.

The remains of a Bo Tree shrine are marked by a small building west of the Vatadage.

The Thuparama, in the south-west corner of the quadrangle, is the best preserved building in Polonnaruwa. Its brick walls are about 7 ft (2 m) thick, and are corbelled overhead to form a vault. The inner sanctum's focal point is a ruined Buddha image, which is said to have had gems for eyes that sparkled with the sun's rays through the skylight.

To the east of the Hatadage is the Gal Pota or "Stone Book", Sri Lanka's longest stone inscription. Besides exalting King Nissanka Malla, the inscription sets forth decrees and also informs us that this slab (weighing 25 tons) was brought all the way from Mihintale around 45 miles (72 km) away!

Gal Pota

Next to the Chapter House north of the Gal Pota is the fascinating Satmahal Prasada. Not much is known about this building. Its current name translates as "Palace of Seven Storeys" and the masonry technique dates from the 12th century. This unusual stepped pyramidal form has been compared to the structure referred to as Ku Kut in Lamphun, northern Thailand.

Satmahal Prasada

Vesak is the first full-moon in May which celebrates Lord Buddha's birth, attainment of Buddhahood and also His entering into Nirvana.

Further north of the Quadrangle, a turning to the right leads to the Pabalu Vihara (7), a brick dagoba dating from the period of Parakramabahu and possibly built in memory of Queen Rupavati, one of the King's consorts.

At the end of this road is another Shiva Devale (8), a small building completely of stone, probably built by the South Indian Cholas in the 11th century. The ruins of the other Hindu temples stand near the ancient stone slabs of the city's northern gateway and a footpath leads to the Menik Vihara (9). This ruined temple is notable for the terracotta lions on its base. An image house with standing Buddha sculptures is also nearby.

Most of Polonnaruwa's great monastic complexes stood to the north of the city.

The first to be encountered along this road is the Alahana Pirivena, whose most notable monument is Nissanka Malla's 12th century Rankot Vihara (10). More than 180 ft (55 m) high, it is the largest dagoba in Polonnaruwa. It was modelled after the water bubble-shaped Ruwanweli Seya of Anuradhapura.

The Buddha Sima Pasada (11), or convocation hall, is the highest structure of the Alahana Pirivena complex. The solemn rites of the monastery were celebrated in this building, and the strict disciplinary code of the Sangha was enforced here.

By far the most striking of the Alahana Pirivena ruins is the image house called Lankatilaka (12). Built by Parakramabahu, this massive brick building of five storeys stood 55 ft (17 m) tall. Within the great nave, interior walls still show traces of the brilliant murals that once adorned them. Worshippers entering the image house had an unobstructed view of a gigantic standing Buddha made of brick (now headless) which dominates the shrine. A vaulted dome above the inner sanctum has collapsed.

To the north of the Lankatilaka is the Kiri Vihara (13), a milk-white dagoba thought to have been built in memory of Queen Subhadra, one of King Parakramabahu's consorts. This is the best preserved dagoba in Polonnaruwa. Its original plaster is largely intact. Small brick mounds around the platform of the dagoba are probably funerary dagobas for the cremated remains of important monks or members of the royal family.

Of all the wonderful structures at Polonnaruwa, the best known are the Buddha sculptures comprising the Gal Vihara (14), Parakramabahu's northern monastery simply meaning "rock shrine". The four 12th century statues, cut from a single granite wall, rank among the true masterpieces of Sri Lankan art.

From the left, the first Buddha image is seated in deep meditation, with legs crossed and hands laid palm upwards on His lap. His head is crowned with a halo and His throne is adorned with lions and thunderbolts. The second sculpture is within a cave hewn from the solid rock. Various deities, including Brahma and Vishnu, surround the image of the seated Buddha. Remains of bright murals that once decorated the cave walls are still visible.

The third figure depicts a 23 ft (7 m) high Buddha image standing on a lotus plinth in the rare cross-armed blessing posture. The face serene and the body relaxed, it was once believed to represent the Buddha's favourite disciple, Ananda.

The fourth statue is a 46 ft (14 m) reclining Buddha, with eyes half-closed and feet slightly askew, representing the moment of entry into Nirvana. His head rests upon His hand, causing a slight depression in the pillow.

North of the Gal Vihara are several additional points of interest. The Demala Maha Seya (15) is a vast artificial hill, a failed attempt by Parakramabahu I to build the world's largest dagoba. A small dagoba of later date crowns the mound.

Further north is the late 12th century Lotus Pond (16), a unique stone bath with five concentric tiers of eight-petalled lotuses.

The Tivanka Image House (17), located at the end of the northern road, is in the same style as the Thuparama or the Lankatilaka. Its main image is a standing Buddha in the "tivanka" or "thrice-bent" position, with shoulders, waist and knee set in opposite directions to symbolise ease and grace, a pose usually reserved for female figures. Timeworn wall paintings within the image house display scenes of the Buddha's previous incarnations. Stucco ornamentation on the outer walls depicts lions and playful dwarves in amusing poses.

In 1982, the ancient city of Polonnaruwa was designated a World Heritage Site by UNESCO.

Parakrama Samudra

Moonstone

The moonstone, a polished semi-circular slab of richly carved granite, is an important example of pure Buddhist art. Moonstones are found at the base of stairways to shrines or at entrances to important buildings.

The layers of concentric rings represent the Buddhist view of life; birth, disease, old age and death. The outermost ring of stylised flames symbolises desire and the state of the world.

සඳකඩ පහන

Of the band of animals portrayed, the elephants represent birth, the lions illness, the horses old age, and the bulls death. These persist in an endless cycle, signifying the continuous rebirth to which all beings are subject to in search of enlightenment.

The band of twisting creepers represent the entangled life force. The serpent is symbolic of lust and the goose purity. The central lotus flower symbolises the state of Nirvana.

Dambadeniya

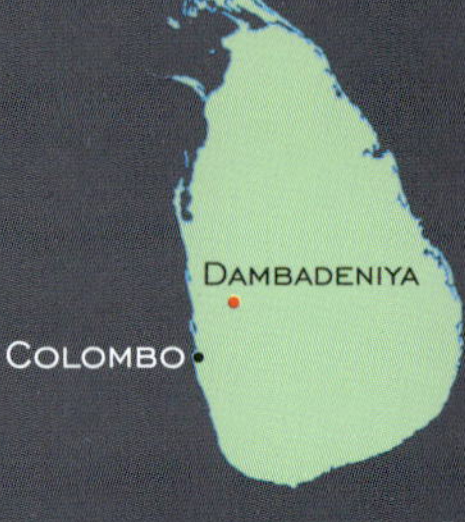

දඹදෙණි රාජධානිය

N 07° 22' 02"
E 80° 09' 00"

With the fall of the Polonnaruwa Kingdom in 1215, King Vijayabahu III (1220-36) fought off the invaders and established Dambadeniya as the Capital of the Island in 1232. He built his palace at Maliga Gala at Dambadeniya rock, defended by outer walls at the base of the rock and made secure by a moat and a series of stone rampart walls which encircled the summit. In his name was created the great monastic complex called Vijayasundararamaya.

Vijayabahu's eldest son King Parakramabahu II (1236-1270) continued his father's religious work, and on ascending the throne encouraged a renaissance in art, literature, and education, promoting religious and economic regeneration in the country. He also brought the Sacred Tooth Relic to Dambadeniya and built a three storeyed Dalada Maligawa (Temple of the Tooth) to house and venerate it. The present temple consists of two terraces, and adjoining it is the Mandapaya where the Tooth Relic was displayed during festivals. Another structure on the terrace is the Kuludage, a roofed stupa house containing Buddhist relics.

King Parakramabahu abdicated in 1270 in favour of his eldest son Vijayabahu IV (1270-1272) who was followed by his younger brother Bhuvanekabahu I (1272-1284) who moved the capital from Dambadeniya to Yapahuwa.

YAPAHUWA

N 07° 49' 00"
E 80° 18' 39"

Bhuvanekabahu I (1272-1284) considered Dambadeniya to be insecure from foreign invasion so in the year 1273 he transferred his Capital to Yapahuwa.

Built around a huge granite rock rising 300 ft (90 m) above the surrounding lowlands, the rock fortress of Yapahuwa would serve as a palace with a military stronghold against invaders. Several caves around the rock containing Buddha images and Brahmi script suggest that this site had been used for centuries as a Buddhist monastery. External fortification includes ramparts and a moat at the base of the rock.

Three steep flights of stone stairs will lead you up the rock. The third flight, ornately decorated with carvings of dancers, elephants and goggle-eyed lions, brings you to an impressive doorway opening onto a terrace where once stood the Palace and the Dalada Maligawa (Temple of the Tooth) which housed the Sacred Tooth Relic.

A path leading to the summit, past a cave and water tank, reveals remains of a small Dagoba and a Bodhi Tree enclosure with superb views of the surrounding countryside.

Yapahuwa served as the capital of Sri Lanka till the death of Bhuvanekabahu in 1284.

Stairway to Heaven

N 07° 58′ 44″
E 80° 50′ 56″

MINNERIYA NATIONAL PARK

About 15 miles (25 km) northwest of Polonnaruwa is Minneriya National Park. Dominated by an ancient reservoir, the Minneriya Wewa built in the 3rd century AD by King Mahasena (274-301), the park is the site of one of the planet's greatest annual spectacles.

Sri Lanka has the highest density of Asian elephants in the world. From February, as the climate becomes drier and waters recede in other areas, elephants migrate to the shores of the Minneriya Wewa.

The Gathering

මින්නේරිය ජාතික වනෝද්‍යානය

By July, there may be as many as 150 elephants congregating, and by September the number may reach up to 300. This is the largest gathering of Asian elephants in the world and is known as 'The Gathering'.

The park is also an important habitat for the Sri Lankan leopard, sloth bear and two endemic monkeys; the purple-faced langur and the toque macaque. In addition to being home to many migrating birds there are also many reptiles including land and water monitors and the Mugger Crocodile.

N 07° 57′ 23″
E 80° 45′ 34″

SIGIRIYA

සීගිරිය

Sigiriya is possibly the most spectacular sight in Sri Lanka. This magnificent, massive monolith rises 600 feet (183 m) from the lush jungle and was one of the most beautiful royal cities that ever graced the earth. Today, the "Lion Rock" is one of the best-preserved and most elaborate surviving urban sites in South Asia and frequently referred to as the eighth wonder of the world.

Lion Rock

King Dhatusena (AD 459-477) who ruled from Anuradhapura had two sons, Kasyapa and Mugalan. Both claimed the right to succeed to their father's throne. Kasyapa was the elder son but his mother was a palace courtesan. Mugalan was the preferred choice, since his mother was the King's consort.

In AD 477, Kasyapa killed his father and seized the throne. Mugalan fled to India, vowing to take revenge. Haunted by the threat of invasion by his brother, Kasyapa spent seven years building an impregnable citadel and beautiful palace on the huge rock of Sigiriya.

In AD 495 when Mugalan returned with his army, Kasyapa descended from his fortress and mounted an elephant to lead the fight against the invasion. At the height of the battle, Kasyapa's elephant, sensing a hidden swamp, turned back. Kasyapa's army thought that their leader was retreating, and so surrendered. Colourful to the last, and realising that he had been defeated, Kasyapa took out his sword and cut off his own head. Taking his rightful place as King, Mugalan returned to Anuradhapura and so Sigiriya's brief 18-year period as the Sinhalese capital was over.

As Sigiriya is situated in the middle of very flat land, any invaders approaching could be seen for miles. Kasyapa was paranoid about his security so he built a wall around the rock and encircled it with a crocodile-filled moat. Massive boulder-catapults, wedged with stone supports, were strategically positioned high around the rock, ready to be sent tumbling down on any invaders.

Close to the main western entrance to Sigiriya are the Water Gardens, symmetrically planned pavilions with gardens, fountains and ponds. Water is scarce in this dry zone, but amazingly these skilled early engineers were able to channel and conserve water and even utilise it for ornamental fountains.

To reach the steps for the climb, one well worn path will take you via the boulder garden, a cluster of rocks including the Preaching Rock which has tiered platforms for preaching monks and rows of notches to hold oil lamps. The Cobra Hood rock has a drip ledge inscription dating from the 2nd century BC, and faint remains of ancient paintings can be seen on the ceiling.

The Cistern and the Audience Hall rocks are part of a single massive boulder which has been split perfectly using fire and water. The exposed surface has a throne at one end and is known as the Audience Hall, while the upper part of the standing half retained a water reservoir.

The stairway through the Elephant Gate leads to the spiral staircase which ascends to the Fresco Gallery, housing the exquisite paintings of the Sigiriya Maidens. Painted in brilliant colours around the rock were a series of charming frescoes of beautiful girls. It is widely believed that these were portraits of Kasyapa's concubines, captured by his best artists for him to enjoy from around his palace gardens. Others believe, because of the heavenly nature of the maidens floating in the clouds, that these superb images are "Apsaras" or celestial nymphs.

Only 21 well preserved frescoes remain of the original 500 or so. Monks who inhabited the rock from the time of the demise of the city may have been responsible for the destruction of the other paintings. Photography is allowed but, to preserve the frescoes, the use of flash is prohibited.

Beyond the spiral staircase, the path is protected on one side by a highly polished plaster Mirror Wall. This was implicitly for the King to admire himself as he ascended to his Summer Palace. The wall was coated with egg white, lime and honey, and is still very reflective. Sightseers from the 7th to the 10th centuries wrote Sinhala verse or "graffiti" on these walls, inspired by the Sigiriya Maidens. The pathway and steps lead onto a plateau.

Overlooking the Lion Terrace once sat the magnificent, gigantic lion that gave the rock its name. Only the paws remain today. This remarkable piece of architecture had steps leading up between the paws and a dramatic entrance to the palace through the mouth of the lion. This sculpture would have been quite breathtaking and perhaps served to remind all of who was the supreme master of the lion race!

Today on the terrace opposite the lion's paws is a large wire cage. This is your only protection against the large bees that very occasionally swarm the rock. Their nests can be seen around the rock, and many attempts have been made to relocate them. However, the bees always return. Many believe that the bees are reincarnations of the many thousands who lost their lives building the magnificent fortress and that they have returned to protect it!

The final stage of the climb to the summit takes you through the lion's paws up a series of metal staircases and across a sequence of steps cut into the side of the rock, flanked by a railing.

The summit covers nearly three acres (just over a hectare) and once accommodated the Royal Summer Palace. The foundations of the palace, a granite throne, dancing terraces, a pool, drinking water tanks, sleeping quarters for the concubines and a flower garden, are all that remain of this marvel. From here, there are superb views of the water gardens and surrounding moat, as well as the beautiful countryside.

Positioned around the rock are little vantage caves which were manned continuously. Soldiers would be lowered by rope to sit perched on these ledges as lookouts for invaders. Falling asleep on the job would be punishable by death, as the guard would literally "drop off".

Kasyapa spent 18 glorious years at Sigiriya, and left a remarkable legacy that is probably for many the most memorable sight they will witness during their stay in Sri Lanka. Not surprisingly, in 1982 the ancient city of Sigiriya was designated a World Heritage Site by UNESCO.

Pidurangala Sigiri Raja Maha Vihara

N 07° 57' 57"
E 80° 45' 44"

පිදුරංගල රජ මහ විහාරය

Adjacent to Sigiriya, is a pyramidal-shaped formation called Pidurangala Rock. Pidurangala and Sigiriya are both linked geographically and historically. Like Sigiriya, Pidurangala was also inhabited by monks from the 3rd century BC. It came into prominence when King Kasyapa commandeered Sigiriya for his Palace. To re-house the monks who were already living there, he gifted them Pidurangala, which translates as 'Offering of the Golden Rock Monastery'.

Pidurangala is not as high as Sigiriya and has steps most of the way, but the final stage of the climb involves scaling some large-scale boulders. It is believed that Kasyapa was cremated here, with his ashes buried in a stupa at the summit. After Kasyapa's death, many monks returned to the rock of Sigiriya but Pidurangala continued to be inhabited by monks as well. The structures at the base are part of the Pidurangala complex built around the Sigiriya period. A cobbled path and a flight of steps lead up to the holy site to a level area which houses quarters for the monks and a Bo Tree. From this point, another flight of steps ascends the rock to a plateau, and the sacred temple of Pidurangala which is built around the cave of an enormous boulder. A section of the outer surface of the boulder has clearly been chiselled away revealing the lighter colour of the exposed rock; this was a common practice known as a 'drip ledge', employed to stop water from entering the cave. There is also an inscription on the drip ledge written in an ancient script.

Golden Rock Monastery

The path to Pidurangala's summit consists mostly of steps cut into the rock. The stairs are surrounded by thick foliage and boulders of all shapes and sizes, covered in a light green moss. Along a long ridge, there is a series of caves under the overhanging rock; One cave houses a 42 ft (13 m) long statue of a reclining Buddha constructed of brick and plaster.

Around 1500 years old, this statue depicts a sleeping Buddha, and not a Buddha entering into Nirvana. A sleeping Buddha has the feet in line and the eyes closed, while the Buddha entering Nirvana, has the feet slightly askew and the eyes half-closed.

Further up from the Buddha statue is a small reservoir which had been cut into the rock and filled with water. This ancient pond held drinking water for the monks.

The last part of the climb is by far the most difficult, but for climbers, the most fun, as they would have to haul themselves over a series of large boulders in order to reach the summit. This final hike will lead you to a small plateau just below the summit, with a short final incline taking you to the summit of Pidurangala, a large flat area which slopes downward towards the back of the rock, offering unrivalled views of the awe-inspiring and magnificent Sigiriya rock.

Cave Temple

The Golden Temple Of Dambulla

N 07° 51′ 58″
E 80° 39′ 07″

රංගිරි දඹුළු විහාරය

One of the most beautiful cave temples in Sri Lanka is the Golden Temple in Dambulla, situated 12 miles (20 km) southwest of Sigiriya. In 1991 the Golden Temple was designated a World Heritage Site by UNESCO. The cave's history dates back to 103 BC, when King Vattagamani Abhaya took refuge there after being driven out of Anuradhapura by a South Indian invasion. After regaining the throne in 89 BC, King Vattagamani Abhaya converted the five caves into shrines in thanks to Lord Buddha. Subsequent kings made further, significant improvements to this magnificent rock temple.

Visitors follow a path with short flights of steps, about half-an-hour's walk, to the caves, which are around two-thirds of the way up the massive 500 ft (150 m) granite rock.

Within the caves are impressive collections of Buddha images. The walls and ceilings are covered with frescoes depicting scenes from the life of Lord Buddha.

Ibbankatuwa Megalithic Tombs

Prehistoric Tombs

Located 3 miles (5 km) southwest of Dambulla, near the Ibbankatuwa water tank, lies an ancient burial site discovered in 1970 by the Archaeological Department. The Ibbankatuwa Tombs date back to Sri Lanka's megalithic prehistoric period, between 700-450 BC.

Excavations between 1988 and 1990 unearthed a cluster of 21 burial chambers radio carbon dated to 600 BC. Further exploration revealed an additional 47 burials. Each tomb, mostly rectangular, contains terracotta pots where cremated ashes and other personal artefacts, are enclosed within four side slab stones and covered by a cap stone.

This burial method had been commonly practised concurrently in European, South East Asian and South Indian regions.

නාලන්ද ගෙඩිගේ

N 07° 40′ 11″
E 80° 38′ 44″

NALANDA GEDIGE

At the geographical centre on the island of Sri Lanka lies a unique edifice created around the 7th century AD.

This well-preserved stone temple, located about 16 miles (25 km) south of Dambulla, has composite styles of architecture: a fusion of Hindu and Buddhist cultures blended together.

Not much is known of Nalanda Gedige, and much remains a mystery. However, it is a legacy of ancient civilisations and is testament to Sri Lanka's rich cultural heritage.

Elite GUIDE
Ancient Temple

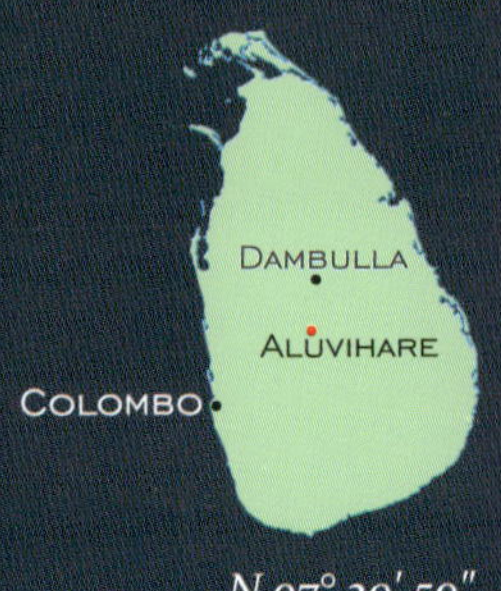

N 07° 29′ 50″
E 80° 37′ 18″

මාතලේ
අලුවිහාරය

Aluvihare Rock Temple

Situated on the Matale-Dambulla road about 28 miles (45 km) south of Dambulla is the Aluvihare Rock Temple, one of the most important temples in the Buddhist faith.

From the day that Mahinda introduced Buddhism to the Island in 247 BC, the forty-year reign of King Devanampiya Tissa (250-210 BC) saw the permanent establishment of Buddhism as the national faith. The whole Island had become the scene of religious activity, including the Temple, Dagoba building and planting the Bo sapling at Aluvihare.

Around 103 BC King Vattagamani Abhaya was chased out of Anuradhapura by seven South Indians, and the country was devastated by war and famine. For fourteen years Vattagamani Abhaya hid himself in the caves of Dambulla, and when he returned to the throne in 89 BC, he converted the caves into shrines in thanks to Lord Buddha. During the time Vattagamani Abhaya was in exile, many thousands of monks perished and the temples were deserted. The future of Buddhism was in danger. The continuation of the three Pitakas brought by Mahinda which had been handed down orally was no longer possible, and it became increasingly vital to preserve the teachings of the Buddha.

Monks assembled at the Aluvihara Temple, and for the first time in history, committed to writing the whole of the Pali Canon, the Tripitaka, the very words of the Buddha, on ola (palm) leaves in Sinhalese for the benefit of mankind.

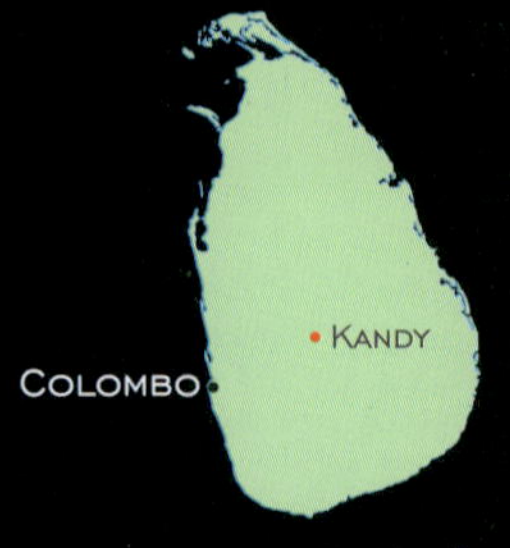

N 07° 17' 37"
E 80° 38' 29"

Nestling amidst low hills, the city of Kandy is a charming combination of valleys, rivers, lakes and waterfalls. It stands as one of the most important symbols of Sinhalese national identity.

Kandy, the second largest city in Sri Lanka, is located 1,600 ft (490 m) above sea level and is therefore not as hot or humid as other parts of the island. Picturesquely set around the banks of a tree-lined lake, it is regarded as the home of arts and crafts, music, dance and song.

Originally known as Senkadagala after the Brahmin hermit Senkada who resided here in a cave, this site was to become the last capital of the Sinhalese kings. The name Kandy was given by the colonial rulers deriving from the Sinhala word "Kanda" meaning hill. To the locals Kandy is known as Maha Nuwara, "Great City", or simply Nuwara.

Royal City

The city was founded by Vikramabahu (1469-1511), and, following the destruction of Kotte, the capital was transferred to Kandy in 1592, during the reign of Vimala Dharma Suriya I (1591-1604).

The Kandyan Kingdom was the thorn in the side of the island's colonial masters, who were unable to gain a hold over the capital, mainly because of its position surrounded by mountains.

The Portuguese had arrived on the island in 1505 after being accidentally blown off course. A few years later, they sought to establish a fortified trading settlement. Their aim was purely commercial; to take control of the island's cinnamon trade, using their sea power to dominate and subdue the territory.

By the 17th century, the Kandyans were distressed at the religious intolerance of the Portuguese (who were gradually taking over the island), so when the Dutch arrived in 1656, they helped in the overthrow of the Portuguese. However, by the time the British arrived in 1796, the Kandyans were disenchanted with the Dutch rulers and were therefore willing to assist the British in their campaign to take over control of the island.

Even in 1802, when the British declared Ceylon a Crown Colony, the Kandyan Kingdom still remained. It was not until 1815, when the last king to rule Sri Lanka, Sri Vikrama Rajasinha (1798-1815) was finally exiled, that the last bastion of Buddhist political power against the colonial masters was subdued.

Ceylon remained a colony of the British Empire until it achieved independence in 1948.

The Kandyans were able to preserve their culture more effectively than in other parts of the island, and their traditions became synonymous with Sinhalese nationalism. Most importantly, within Kandy resides the symbol of Sri Lanka's sovereignty, preserved in its own temple the Dalada Maligawa "Temple of the Tooth", the sacred Tooth of Lord Buddha.

In 1988, the sacred city of Kandy was designated a World Heritage Site by UNESCO.

Temple Of The Tooth

දළදා මාලිගාව

One of the most famous attractions in Sri Lanka, overlooking the Kandy Lake with its golden roof, is the Temple of the Tooth, "Sri Dalada Maligawa".

After Lord Buddha passed away into Nirvana in 483 BC, some important relics, including His begging bowl, His collarbone and some strands of His hair, were recovered from His funeral pyre and later sent to Sri Lanka to be placed within the inner sanctums of dagobas built for them. Lord Buddha's Tooth was also recovered and kept in the Indian Kingdom of Kalinga. The Tooth was considered the most sacred relic of Buddhism.

In the 4th century AD, due to the resurgence of Hinduism, the future of the Tooth was thrown into doubt. In AD 331 the Indian king sent the Tooth to Sri Lanka, hidden in the hair of his daughter Princess Hemamala accompanied by Prince Danta.

The sacred Tooth relic became not only the most precious icon of Sinhalese pride but also a symbol of kingship. It was customary for the kings to build a temple for the Tooth relic near their palace, and to become its custodian.

Vimala Dharma Suriya I (1591-1604) brought the Tooth relic to Kandy and built a two-storey shrine. Improvements were made by subsequent kings. Sri Vikrama Rajasinha (1798-1815) built the elegant Pattirippuwa, the temple's octagonally-shaped building (which today houses the library) and also constructed the beautiful artificial lake beside the temple, which Kandy is centred around.

Few people ever see the Tooth relic itself. Most will see the great dagoba-shaped Karanduwa, a golden reliquary, which is the outermost casket of seven. Within, the six increasingly smaller shrines are also of pure gold and ornamented with precious gems.

The Karanduwa is housed in the Sanctuary of the Udmale, the upper chamber of the two-tiered inner shrine. The sanctuary is opened at dawn, with ceremonies starting at 5:30am, 9:30am and 6:30pm, when the temple comes alive with drumming, clouds of incense and the constant procession of pilgrims carrying floral offerings, filing past an open window in order to catch a glimpse of the reliquary inside.

The hall behind the Shrine has a number of golden Buddha statues and paintings depicting the life of the Buddha and the arrival of Buddhism to the island.

Next to the Temple is the Audience Hall (1784) with ornate wooden pillars and stone floor where Kandyan kings held court. The historic document ending the Kandyan Kingdom and handing the territory over to the British was signed here in 1815.

On the southern side of the Temple, facing the lake, is an open courtyard where elephants are adorned for the most unique and magnificent annual festival – the Esala Perahera.

The Esala Perahera

ඇසළ පෙරහැර

Every year, during the lunar month of Esala (July/August), the romantic city of Kandy hosts Asia's most spectacular festival, the Esala Perahera, in honour of the island's most important possession, Lord Buddha's Tooth.

The Perahera, which means "procession", is a 10-day festival and parade around the city, culminating on "Poya" or full moon. This festival has been taking place annually since the Tooth relic arrived on the island in AD 331, and when the relic was moved to Kandy in 1592, the Perahera moved with it. The rituals and ceremonies associated with the Perahera have persisted throughout the centuries and changed little over time.

Four historic Devales (temples) play an important role in the Perahera alongside the Dalada Maligawa, and for the first five nights the Peraheras are celebrated within their grounds. The most important Devale is dedicated to Vishnu the Hindu deity, located west of the Royal Palace. Opposite the main entrance to the Dalada Maligawa is the Natha Devale, dedicated to Natha, a bodhisattva (Buddha-to-be) and protector of the city of Kandy. South of the Natha Devale is the Pattini Devale. Pattini is the goddess of chastity and health. West of Pattini Devale is the Kataragama Devale dedicated to the god of War.

On the sixth night the Devale Peraheras are joined by the Dalada Maligawa Perahera and from the seventh night onward the procession grows in splendour and length. Leading the procession are whip crackers, and fire acrobats announcing the approach of the Perahera. The Buddhist flag bearers proceed next followed by Chieftains riding dressed elephants accompanied by drummers, flute players and hundreds of Kandyan dancers.

The highlight of the pageant is the sight of the magnificent caparisoned "Maligawa Tusker" carrying the canopied Perahera Karanduwa. As the Tusker majestically moves forward, a white cloth is unrolled before him to walk on. Ancient Peraheras would have paraded the sacred Tooth itself, but today the Tooth does not leave its Temple – not only is the Tooth Sri Lanka's most prized possession, it is also the island's seal of sovereignty.

Peradeniya Botanical Gardens

N 07° 16' 16"
E 80° 35' 43"

Situated about 4 miles (6 km) from Kandy, Peradeniya Botanical Gardens was originally the royal pleasure garden of King Kirti Sri Rajasinha (1747-1782).

During the governorship of Edward Barnes (1824-1831), all botanical experiments on the island were transferred to Peradeniya due to its cooler climate.

In 1839 tea seeds of the Assam jat and young tea plants had been sent from the Botanical Gardens in Calcutta to Peradeniya, and small experimental plantings were carried out over a period of many years.

Today the 147 acres (60 hectares) of gardens, nestled in the sweeping curve of the Mahaweli River, are dedicated to the flora of Sri Lanka and include representative species from all over the tropical world.

The Spice Garden on the right of the main entrance has many exotic specimens and the Orchid House reflects the amazing variety of species to be found in Sri Lanka. The main attraction is the 50-acre (20-hectare) arboretum of around 10,000 trees.

One of the rarest plants in the garden is the Coco de Mer, which has the largest and heaviest fruit in the plant kingdom, weighing on average between 22 and 44 lbs (10 and 20 kg), and taking around 5 years to mature.

The Royal Palm Avenue, the bamboo-fringed River Drive, and Bat Drive where flying foxes hang upside down, are popular with visitors.

Lord Mountbatten found the gardens the perfect location to set up South East Asia Command Headquarters during World War II.

Victoria Golf & Country Club

N 07° 15' 57"
E 80° 46' 23"

Just a short drive from Kandy, next to Victoria Dam, is located the most exquisite Victoria Golf & Country Club.

Landscaped from 500 acres (200 hectares) of farmland and jungle, this most picturesque club has been voted one of the top 100 most beautiful golf courses in the world. Whilst the course is uniquely challenging, you will also appreciate the relaxed atmosphere, rarely found at other golf clubs around the world.

The resort offers luxury chalets in idyllic surroundings with a swimming pool, a tennis court, herbal massage, nature trails and bird watching.

MAHIYANGANA RAJA MAHA VIHARA

මහියංගන රජ මහා විහාරය

N 07° 19' 19"
E 80° 59' 27"

On the banks of the Mahaweli Ganga, in the Badulla district of Uva Province, is the town of Mahiyangana.

Lord Buddha made three visits to the Island of Lanka. His first visit was to Mahiyangana where He settled a dispute between the Yakkas and Nagas, the two tribes inhabiting the Island. After preaching His Dhamma, the Buddha gave a few of His hairs from His head for the people to worship. These hairs were placed in a golden reliquary and enshrined in the island's first ever stupa built to house the relic on the site of the visitation. Over time, a succession of kings renovated the stupa and built edifices for the monks to meditate and preach at this sacred site for Buddhists.

Close to Mahiyangana, Dambana is a quiet jungle village known for its indigenous Veddha tribe. The arrival of the earliest inhabitants of Lanka dates back around 40,000 years; once a powerful community there are now only a few hundred Veddhas that remain.

Nuwara Eliya

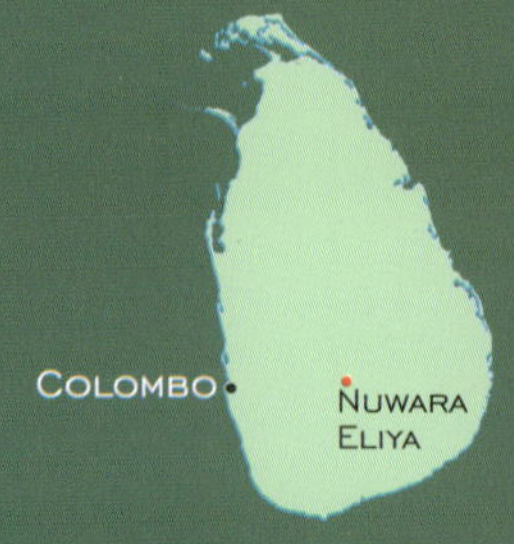

N 06° 57′ 48″
E 80° 46′ 09″

Nuwara Eliya is the capital of the "hill country", which consists of an area that has Kandy on its northern boundary, Badulla to the east, Haputale on the southern side, and the Peak Wilderness Sanctuary incorporating Adam's Peak on the western side.

Overlooked by Pidurutalagala, the island's highest peak at 8,200 ft (2,524 m), Nuwara Eliya, or "City of Lights", is located at 6,199 ft (1,889 m) and is Sri Lanka's highest town, with temperatures averaging 57°F (14°C) throughout the year.

The British discovered Nuwara Eliya early in the 19th century. They thought its climate was ideal, and so decided to use it as a place to retreat from the heat and dust of Colombo.

Plantations

Nuwara Eliya was soon to become their "hill station" and, by the early 20th century, planters, estate managers and senior public servants all built their homes here.

This exclusive colonial resort would naturally take on a quintessentially British feel, and with its Tudor-style black and white houses and immaculate lawns, you could be excused for thinking you were in a suburb of Surrey in the 1930s.

The golf course, founded by the Gordon Highlanders Golf Club on a visit to Nuwara Eliya in 1889, the racecourse, cricket pitches, croquet lawns, tennis courts and gentleman's clubs all bear testament to British patronage.

The British systematically built roads all over Sri Lanka, including making Nuwara Eliya accessible from Colombo, a journey which took the good part of a day.

Nowadays, Nuwara Eliya is quite a busy place and a hub of commercial activity. Sri Lankans from all over the island now use it as their retreat, so weekends and holidays are a busy time.

Coffee Or Tea?

The island's economy under Dutch rule had been dominated by the spice trade. When the British took control at the end of the 18th century, they introduced a plantation economy that proved very successful and Ceylon became a major supplier of raw materials and commodities to the vast imperial market.

Coffee was first introduced into southern India and Ceylon by the Arabs. From 1825 it had been grown successfully on a commercial scale. By the 1860s Ceylon became the world's largest producer of coffee, peaking in 1868. The following year the disease *Hemileia vastatrix*, "coffee rust", was noticed in the estates, and within twenty years completely ruined the thousands of acres of fine coffee.

In December 1839, Dr Wallich, the eminent Indian botanist and director of the Calcutta Botanic Gardens, had sent seeds of the Assam jat and young plants to Peradeniya Botanical Gardens near Kandy. These were followed in February 1840 by 205 plants, and small experimental plantings were carried out. In May, the Superintendent at Peradeniya, Mr Normansell, sent several plants to Nuwara Eliya and a handful of more enterprising coffee planters had cleared the odd half acre and planted tea.

During the coffee boom, and just two years before the coffee leaf disease, the Scottish coffee planter, James Taylor, first commercially planted tea in 1867. Taylor was the innovative Superintendent of Loolecondera Estate, located south-east of Kandy, where he cleared 20 acres of land on a hill slope and planted tea seeds in Field no.7.

The tea plant was growing well in the ideal climate of the hills of Ceylon. Within the first years Taylor was not only able to grow tea on a commercial scale, but also mastered processing it. In 1872 the first shipment of tea to England was recorded. Today, Sri Lanka is one of the world's leading producers of tea.

One lump or two?

Although tea originated in China over 5,000 years ago, it was Ceylon that made tea famous in the 19th and 20th centuries, as Ceylon tea was being used by almost every major tea brand.

Ceylon tea is prized for its unparalleled quality and a variety unmatched, especially for a small island boasting dramatically different teas in different parts of its tea-growing regions.

Ceylon tea is classified by the elevation at which it is grown. The "Low Grown" teas produced in Sri Lanka below 2,000 ft are known for their superior black leaf appearance, which has a reddish brew colour. The "High Grown" teas produced above 4,000 ft are known for their bright colour and brisk aromatic liquors. High grown Ceylon teas do not share the dense, black colour of the low grown leaf, being browner in appearance, but have unsurpassed liquors ranging from a bright golden colour to deep red.

Labour is provided mainly by the now localised descendants of the indentured labourers brought in by the British from South India in the 1820s.

Only leaf buds and young leaves are plucked and used in making tea.

After picking, the leaves are dried to reduce moisture and then rolled to release the leaves' natural juices. This is then left to ferment in a controlled environment before finally being dried in a hot-air chamber.

There are different types and varieties of teas, graded by size of flake and quality. Assessing the quality of tea, professional tea tasters take into consideration the colour, strength, quality, aroma and flavour of the brew as well as the colour of the infused leaf.

As Ceylon tea is unique in quality and flavour and regarded as the finest in the world, Dilmah has pioneered the concept of Single Origin Tea (which was the preferred practice of family owned plantations in the early 1900s) offering consumers a guarantee of consistency, quality and authenticity.

Tea is drunk by about half of the world's population, and with names such as pekoe, orange pekoe, broken orange pekoe etc the best label for this aromatic stimulant has to be – Dilmah Pure Ceylon Tea!

HILL CLUB

N 06° 58' 03"
E 80° 45' 56"

The famous Hill Club was founded in 1876 as a tea planters' club, overlooking a golf course. This 36-roomed club is very traditionally British – members are usually expatriates but some locals are now granted membership. Visitors must become temporary members; men have to wear a jacket and tie.

Dinner is superb, a modern British experience, served by white-gloved waiters in a very formal atmosphere. The billiard room is, in fact, the oldest part of the building, and a game of snooker after dinner is a great way to relax with, of course, the obligatory glass of brandy.

TEA TRAILS

N 06° 51' 04"
E 80° 35' 54"

In central Sri Lanka, just 3 hours from Colombo, lies the Bogawantalawa Valley, the "Golden Valley of Tea" and home to old Ceylon. Here in solitude, at an elevation of 4,000 ft, lies Ceylon Tea Trails, 4 classic colonial bungalows built for British tea estate managers in the days of the Raj. These historic houses have been beautifully restored by Dilmah Tea to offer guests the unique experience of life on a working tea estate. Bungalows range in size from 4 to 6 luxurious rooms and suites.

Unwind in the beautiful gardens, visit a Tea factory or spend an adventure-filled day biking, trekking and white-water rafting. Tea Trails offers an unforgettable holiday that will rejuvenate your spirit in the heart of the magical world of Ceylon tea.

Elite
GUIDE

Horton Plains

N 06° 48′ 28″
E 80° 47′ 14″

The Central Highlands is the newest World Heritage Site in Sri Lanka. Inscribed in 2010, the site incorporates three protected areas; the Peak Wilderness Sanctuary, Horton Plains National Park, and Knuckles Mountain Range.

Horton Plains National Park is located 19 miles (30 km) south of Nuwara Eliya. The plains form an undulating plateau at an altitude of 6,890 ft (2,100 m) and cover an area of over 7,400 acres (3,000 hectares) consisting mainly of grassland interspersed with patches of forest.

The second and third highest mountains in Sri Lanka form part of this region, Kirigalpotta at 7,800 ft (2,387 m) and Thotupola Kanda at 7,730 ft (2,357 m).

හෝර්ටන්තැන්න

Three rivers originate on the plains, the Mahaweli, the Kelani and the Walawe. The most stunning feature of Horton Plains is World's End, a 2.5 mile (4 km) walk, where the southern Horton Plains come to an abrupt end with an almost sheer drop of over 2,600 ft (800 m).

There are fantastic views over the distant hills and valleys, but this can often be obscured by mist, especially during the rainy season from April to September.

Named after Sir Robert Horton (1831-1837), the British Governor at the time, Horton Plains provides a habitat for most of the endemic plants and animals in Sri Lanka and is therefore of considerable natural importance.

Wilderness Sanctuary

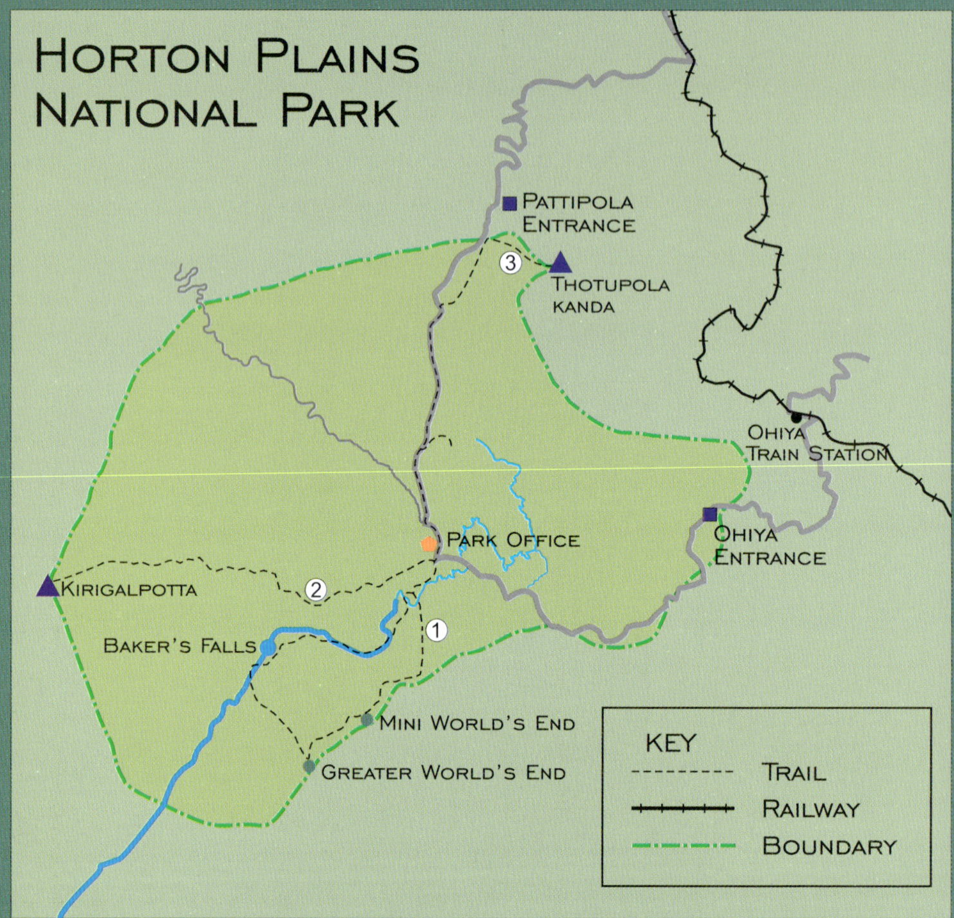

There are three trails within Horton Plains National Park, and it is highly recommended that you hire a local guide in advance, whose extensive knowledge can greatly enhance your trek. One of the best for Horton Plains is Rikaz +94 77 470 3941.

Trail ① To Mini World's End, Greater World's End and Baker's Falls.
This trek is around 5.5 miles (9 km) and a round trip will take about 4 hours.

Trail ② Climbing Kirigalpotta mountain.
This trek is around 11 miles (18 km) and a round trip will take about 7 hours through forest and grasslands. From the summit are panoramic views of Adam's Peak and the southern landscape.

Trail ③ Climbing Thotupola Kanda.
This trek is from Pattipola entrance and a path of about 1 mile (1.6 km) will take you to the starting point of the climb. Steps to the summit will provide fantastic panoramic views of Ohiya and Nuwara Eliya. A round trip will take about 3 hours.

හෝටන්තැන්න
ஹோட்டன்தென்ன
HORTON PLAINS

Elite
GUIDE

ELLA

ඇල්ල

At an elevation of 3,415 ft (1,041 m) in the Badulla district, the charming village of Ella, nestled in the hills with stunning views of the surrounding countryside, has become a popular destination for backpackers and hikers seeking a little adventure.

The best way of getting to Ella is the idyllic train journey with the most spectacular views. The trip from Kandy takes around 7 hours, while the journey from Nanu Oya (Nuwara Eliya) takes around 3 hours. This is considered one of the world's most beautiful train rides.

There is a variety of activities on offer in Ella, from exploring tea plantations and amazing hiking to visiting waterfalls and caves, and enjoying the multitude of cafes, bars and restaurants.

A hike to the top of Little Adam's Peak is a fairly easy climb to a height of 3,743 ft (1,141 m). Following a good path through lush green tea plantations, the trip should take around a couple of hours at a leisurely pace and is well worth it for the 360-degree views.

The trek to Ella Rock which stands at 4,514 ft (1,376 m) is more arduous; a round trip takes about four hours through plantations and dense forest. However, if you're up for the challenge, you will be rewarded not only with the satisfaction of conquering this mountain, but also with stunning views, especially at sunrise.

The most popular attraction for visitors is the iconic Nine Arch Bridge, an engineering marvel.

The Hindu epic, the *Ramayana*, relates that King Ravana of Lanka abducted Indian Prince Rama's wife Sita, and hid her in the cave that is now known as Ravana Cave. Ravana Falls is where it is believed that Sita bathed in a pool that gathered from this waterfall.

Travelling south towards Bandarawela is the Dhowa Rock Temple with a 38 ft (11.5 m) Buddha statue hewn from the rock.

Built in the 1st century BC, this unfinished image was sculpted during the reign of King Vattagamani Abhaya (89-77 BC) who took refuge here after an Indian invasion.

Positioned in the heart of the hill country, amidst captivating scenery, is the enchanting market town of Bandarawela. Its cool climate made it popular with the British colonisers, and the rolling hills, fragrant flowers, tea plantations, and paddy fields make it perfect for nature treks.

An hour from Bandarawela is Haputale. At an elevation of 6,500 ft (1,981 m), offering breath-taking views, is Lipton's seat, a most impressive viewpoint, and once a favourite respite of Sir Thomas Lipton, the tea magnate, where he sat overlooking his estate with an obligatory cup of tea!

At an elevation of 5,150 ft (1,570 m) is St. Benedict's Monastery at Adisham Hall. Constructed in 1931 Adisham was the country house of Sir Thomas Villiers, a British aristocrat and planter.

The Tudor style bungalow, named after Adisham in Kent where Sir Thomas was born, is set upon a cliff surrounded by forests with endless views of undulating hills and valleys.

In 1961 the Sylvestro Benedictine Congregation acquired the stately home and the 10 acre (4 hectare) estate, and converted it into a monastery. This tranquil haven is perfect for a monastic life of solace, quiet reflection and contemplation.

The monastery has beautiful manicured gardens and there is a small shop which sells organic homemade jams, marmalades and chutneys all produced from fruits harvested by the monks from their orchards and the income from sales goes towards maintenance of the monastery.

Buduruwagala

බුදුරුවගල

Located about 18 miles (29 km) south of Ella is the ancient site of Buduruwagala. Cut out of the rock are seven Buddhist images dating back to the 10th century in the Mahayana style of Buddhism. The central Buddha image is 51 ft (15 m) high making it the tallest on the island. The Buddha is depicted in the Abhaya Mudra with His right hand upwards and His palm forward in blessing devotees. It still has traces of an orange pigment on the stucco robe; and square holes cut into the rock above the head indicate that in the past there may have been a canopy adorning the image.

Mahayana Buddhism

The white central image of the three to the left of the Buddha is said to be the Bodhisattva or "enlightened being", Avalokitesvara. The female figure on the right in the "tivanka" or "thrice bent" position with shoulders, waist and knee set in opposite directions to symbolise ease and grace, is thought to be Bodhisattva Tara the consort of Avalokitesvara. The male figure on the left is believed to be their son Prince Sudana. To the right of the main Buddha, the central of the three figures is thought to be Maithri Bodhisattva and on his left is Vajirapani Bodhisattva.

Palk Bay

Jaffna Peninsula

Bay of Bengal
N
Sakkotai
Cape
thurai
Point
Pedro
li
Manatkaadu
Beach
Indian Ocean
Pooneryn
Nallur
Kilinochchi

Jaffna

யாழ்ப்பாணம்

N 09° 39′ 53″
E 80° 01′ 00″

Positioned at the northern tip of Sri Lanka around 190 miles (300 km) north of Colombo, is the Jaffna Peninsula and its surrounding islands.

Jaffna, Sri Lanka's northernmost town and the capital of the Northern Province, is closer to Southern India than Colombo. It has a unique blend of Tamil and Hindu culture along with some old-world colonial charm mixed in.

The earliest settlers, arriving around the 2nd or 3rd century BC, were predominantly Buddhist. The majority of the population, Sri Lankan Tamils, are descendants of Southern Indian invaders of the Pandya, Chola and Pallava Kingdoms of the 2nd and 3rd centuries AD. Today there is a significant number of Sri Lankan Moors, Indian Tamils and other ethnic groups. Most Sri Lankan Tamils are Hindu, but some are Christian. Muslim and Buddhist communities form a minority.

By the 13th century Jaffna had developed into the capital of the powerful Tamil Kingdom known as Jaffnapatam. Its realm expanded to Mannar with its valuable pearl industry and continued south. In the 15th century, the King of Kotte, Parakramabahu VI (1412-67), gained control of the entire north, unifying the island.

The Portuguese first landed in Sri Lanka in 1505, and after forming trading links with the island, they built a small fort in Galle in 1589. In 1619, the Portuguese established a foothold in Jaffna with a permanent fortified settlement, aiming to take over the Kingdom due to its strategic position next to the Palk Strait, which would allow them to control the sea route between east and west India as well as the trade of the pearl industry. By 1621, they had finally seized Jaffna. The Portuguese destroyed many Hindu Temples, and many of the local fishermen were forcefully converted to Catholicism.

In 1658, the Dutch East India Company (VOC) ousted the Portuguese and built an imposing fort over the Portuguese stronghold to protect their trading. The Dutch were more considerate towards the locals, and most of the Hindu temples that the Portuguese destroyed were rebuilt as well as churches and government buildings. During the Dutch period on the Island Jaffna became a prominent trading town.

The Jaffna Peninsula's terrain is very flat and falls under the dry zone, and the north-east monsoon is its main source of rain, lasting from October to late December. Despite limited water resources and poor soil, farmers have developed a highly successful and profitable farming system, rice being the major cultivatable crop.

The Dutch surrendered the fort to the British East India Company in 1796, and under British rule, Jaffna enjoyed a period of rapid growth and prosperity. By building roads and a railway line, the British connected Jaffna to Kandy and Colombo.

Jaffna Mainland

INDEX

1. NALLUR KANDASWAMY KOVIL
2. KING SANGILIYAN'S STATUE
3. THE SANGILIYAN THOPPU
4. YAMUNA ERI
5. MANTRI MANAI
6. KACHCHERI
7. JAFFNA FISH MARKET
8. JAFFNA LIBRARY
9. JAFFNA FORT
10. JAFFNA MARKET
11. CLOCK TOWER
12. JAFFNA ARCHAEOLOGICAL MUSEUM
13. NILAVARAI WELL
14. MANATKAADU BEACH
15. VALLIPURAM
16. ALVAR VISHNU KOVIL
17. POINT PEDRO
18. KANKESANTHURAI BEACH
19. KANKESANTHURAI LIGHTHOUSE
20. KANKESANTHURAI PORT
21. HOT SPRINGS IN KEERIMALAI
22. KEERIMALAI NAGULESWARAM KOVIL
23. KATHURUGODA VIHARAYA, KANTHARODAI
24. DAMBAKOLA PATUNA SANGHAMITTA TEMPLE

Nallur Kandaswamy Kovil (1)

Amongst the countless Hindu kovils in the Northern Province, the most venerated of these sacred abodes is the legendary Nallur Kandaswamy Kovil. The temple was originally founded in 948 AD in Nallur, an area that served as the capital of the Jaffna kings. Due to foreign invasions, the temple had to be relocated several times within the Nallur area. It was rebuilt in the 13th century, but the third incarnation of the temple was destroyed by the Portuguese in 1624, and churches were constructed over the ruins.

The present temple was constructed in 1734 during the Dutch colonial era. Renovations over the years proclaim this temple complex dedicated to Murugan (or Skanda) the God of love, war and beauty, as the most impressive Hindu temple in Sri Lanka, rivalling the great shrines of India.

The main entrance to the temple is on the east side, featuring an ornately carved gopuram (tower) in Dravidian architecture standing five stories high. To the north and south are the temple's most recent additions; two Raja gopurams both in Dravidian style towering around nine stories. The northern gopuram, slightly larger than the southern one, is the largest on the island. Inside the temple, there are numerous shrines with larger-than-life murals, richly decorated golden arched corridors, and a beautiful courtyard with a holy bathing well.

Pujas take place throughout the day, and the temple is frequented by worshippers of all races and religions. Visitors must remove their shoes and men must remove their shirts before entering. The temple is the focus of the spectacular annual Nallur Festival.

Nallur Kandaswamy Temple Festival

During the month of Aadi (July/August), the Nallur Temple hosts its famous festival, the Nallur Kandaswamy Temple Festival. Celebrated over a period of 25 days, this vibrant festival is steeped in rituals and tradition with its elaborate processions and pujas, and is considered the grandest and most venerated of all. Attended by tens of thousands of worshippers, men dressed in crisp white sarongs and ladies draped in their beautiful bright saris, transform the entire temple complex into a vast sea of colour.

Amidst the religious ceremonies is the daily procession of the idol of Lord Murugan or his holy vel (spear-like weapon), carried in revered chariots in the form of animals (peacock, cobra or swan) and accompanied by images of the deity's consorts, Devasena and Valli, around the inner and outer precincts of the kovil.

Of the rituals, the festival held on the 24th day, the 'Ther Festival' is the most popular. Here the 'Ther' or silver chariot carrying the statue of God Murugan and his consorts, dressed in splendid attire, is carried on the shoulders of thousands of devotees and paraded along the temple streets accompanied by drumming and the chanting "Aro Haram".

Some devotees offer their respect by rolling on the ground around the temple. Many devotees, mainly men, perform elaborate ceremonies and rigorous Kavadi dances. Kavadi is a physical burden undertaken as an act of penance to invoke blessings or in thanksgiving for the fulfilment of vows. Many carry on their shoulders, a semi-circular decorated canopy supported by a wooden rod; some even have a small spear through their tongue or cheeks. Other types of Kavadi involve the ritualistic practice of hooks pieced into the backs of entranced devotees and suspended and swung from a decorated bullock cart or tractor.

The final ritual of the 25-day festival is the holy wedding, where the matrimony between Murugan and Valli, and Murugan and Devasena, is re-enacted.

The annual Nallur festival is a religious inspiration to all Hindus. In attendance are devotees from around the island and around the world irrespective of ethnicity, creed or religion, all united in seeking spiritual enlightenment.

King Sangiliyan's Statue (2)

Close to Nallur Kandaswamy Kovil is a statue is dedicated to King Cankili II (1617-1619) the last King of Jaffna.

This serves as an important landmark in Jaffna.

Sangiliyan Thoppu (3)

Further north, one can find the relic of an ancient arch that was once part of the outer facade of the palace of the King of Jaffna. Following the execution of the king by the Portuguese, the palace was destroyed, leaving all but the foundations and the facade.

Yamuna Eri (4)

Yamuna Eri is a U-shaped pond situated behind the Sangiliyan Thoppu, and it is believed to have been the Queens bathing pool. Built by King Cinkai Ariyan Cekaracacekaran I (1215–1240), it would have been part of the same palace complex of the ancient kingdom. It is believed that the King brought water from the Yamuna River in India to fill this pool.

Mantri Manai (5)

Even further north are the remains of a palatial residence known as Mantri Manai.

This was believed to have been the home of a Minister during the reign of King Cankili II (1617-1619) the last King of the Jaffna Kingdom.

Kachcheri (6)

A kachcheri or district secretariat is the principal government department that administrates an area while liaising with the central government. The Jaffna Kachcheri was built in the 19th century within the 27 acre (11 hectare) gardens and grounds known as Old Park which also houses the palatial residence of the British Government Agent for the Northern Province, Percival Acland Dyke.

Jaffna Fish Market (7)

Located on Reclamation Road right on the shore of the lagoon, the Jaffna Fish Market is a colourful, bustling hive of activity. Early morning, after a night of fishing, the fishermen deliver their fresh catch to the market for the locals to buy.

With individual stalls set up randomly on the ground of this vibrant open-air hub, a wide variety of seafood is on offer, from tiny sprats, squid, crabs, prawns, lobster to larger fish with exotic names. Vendors rhythmically shout out their wares to potential buyers and after a bit of haggling the fish is weighed using rudimentary scales and then skilfully gutted and filleted.

Jaffna Library (8)

The Jaffna library was originally built in 1933. Containing over 97,000 books and manuscripts, including seminal texts on Sri Lankan history and culture, much written on palm leaf manuscripts, it was once considered one of the largest collections in Asia. The library sadly was burnt down in 1981 during the civil conflict.

In 2001, the library was restored extensively keeping the elegant original neo-Mughal design. A new complex was added and thousands of new books were introduced. Today the library stands as a symbol of Tamil pride and culture.

Jaffna Fort (9)

One of the most popular attractions in Jaffna overlooking the Jaffna lagoon, a legacy of a colonial past, is the magnificent Dutch fort.

Originally built by the Portuguese in 1619, the fort was square shaped with bastions at each corner and surrounded by a moat.

In 1658, after a three-month siege, the Dutch captured the fort and ousted the Portuguese. The Dutch then expanded the fort in the shape of a five-pointed star in the classic style of Dutch architecture.

The fort occupies 62 acres (25 hectares) and was built using limestone and coral stone. It housed five ramparts, artillery fortifications, administrative garrisons, Groote Kerk - a Dutch church dating from 1706, a prison, a hospital, the Queen's House - former residence of the Dutch and British Governors, a small house once occupied by the author Leonard Woolf as well as 21 dug wells. There are also three drawbridges connecting the outer fortification and the inner fort.

The Dutch surrendered the fort to the British East India Company in 1796, and it remained a British garrison up until Independence in 1948.

Jaffna Market (10)

A great way to sample the daily life of the locals is to visit the local market place - and Jaffna Market, situated at the junction of KKS road and Hospital Road, is unique. Numerous open-air pavilions boast the vendors extensive array of colourful, locally grown and exotic fruit and vegetables in all shapes and sizes. The freshly picked produce is weighed with basic scales and packaged for the customer in a banana leaf.

Jaffna curry powder is legendary, and the market stocks all the spices needed to create this fiery concoction including fennel, turmeric, coriander, cumin, sun-dried chillies, fenugreek and cinnamon. You can pick and mix to your own family recipe or buy a readymade mixture off the shelf. Popular with the locals are the sweet treats unique to Jaffna, made from the sap of the Palmyra tree. In addition, the market offers an eclectic mix of other products including hand-crafted household items made of palmyra leaf, apparel, ornaments, and even gold jewellery.

Clock Tower (11)

Built in 1875 in honour of the visit of Queen Victoria's eldest son, Prince Albert Edward, the clock tower is unique in design, with a Moorish domed top.

The Prince of Wales had embarked on an extensive tour of the Indian Subcontinent and spent seven days touring Sri Lanka.

Jaffna Archaeological Museum (12)

Established in 1978 and situated on Navalar Road, is the Archaeological Museum. The museum houses a collection of Buddhist and Hindu antiquities discovered around the Jaffna Peninsula. Of the rich historical tapestry on show are artefacts made of metal, wood, stone and ivory. In addition, there is a variety of coins found locally.

Exhibits from excavations at Kantharodai including Buddha statues, a 7-mouthed pot, and a stone pillar with an inscription in Prakrit are also on display here.

Other items include a wooden palanquin, a few Dutch cannons, a whale bone and many more curios. Opening hours are from 08:30 am to 4:30 pm.

NILAVARAI WELL (13)

Located in Puttur, 8.5 miles (14 km) northeast of Jaffna town, the Nilavarai Well is the largest natural freshwater waterhole on the Jaffna Peninsula. Local people believe the well to be bottomless, and never drying up even during severe droughts. This has been a sacred place since ancient times; some believe that the well was created by Lord Rama, and others believe it was created by Hanuman the Hindu Monkey God.

MANATKAADU BEACH (14)

Located on the Bay of Bengal, southeast of Point Pedro, is a pristine stretch of sand with crystal-clear waters. Surrounded by large sand dunes, Manatkaadu Beach is inhabited by a small fishing community who can be seen daily hauling in their catch. With its natural beauty and tranquil ambiance, this beach is a great choice to get away from the hustle and bustle of life.

Vallipuram (15)

Vallipuram is an ancient village east of Point Pedro where rich archaeological discoveries were found indicating an early settlement and Buddhist civilisation.

In 1936, a 2nd century gold sheet known as Vallipuram Ran Sannasa was discovered beneath the foundation of an ancient structure. It records the construction of a Buddhist Viharaya during the reign of King Vasabha (67-111). Other items found were some funerary urns, bricks, pottery, coins and a Buddha image.

Alvar Vishnu Kovil (16)

Vallipuram is also home to an ancient Hindu temple, Alvar Vishnu Kovil, The temple, constructed around the 13th century is dedicated to Lord Vishnu. Inside, colourful images depict stories relating to the divine powers of Lord Vishnu, the preserver and protector of the universe.

The annual 17-day festival of the Kovil is held in the months of September / October during which an image of Vishnu is taken out on a daily procession. Interestingly an image of Vallipuram's Alvar Vishnu Temple appears on Sri Lanka's One Thousand Rupee note.

Point Pedro (17)

Sri Lanka's northernmost town is Point Pedro. Point Pedro is a corruption of the Portuguese "Ponta das Pedras" meaning "rocky cape" descriptive of its natural features. With its stony coast, pristine beaches and turquoise water Pont Pedro was a fishing and trading port in ancient times.

Geographically, the northernmost point of the teardrop isle is Sakkotai Cape. On the north eastern corner is the lighthouse built by the British in 1916. The tower is 105 ft (32 m) and warns mariners of the dangerous shallows and rocky coast.

Kankesanthurai Beach (18)

Kankesanthurai beach is one of the best beaches in the Northern Province. A perfect sandy beach with palm trees and cool water, an ideal spot to get away.

Kankesanthurai Lighthouse (19)

In 1893 the British constructed the Kankesanthurai Lighthouse with an octagonal tower at a height of 72 ft (22 m).

Kankesanthurai Port (20)

Located on the northern coast is the port of Kankesanthurai, one of the island's ancient trading ports which served as a gateway for trade globally. With its ancient temples, the port at Kankesanthurai has attracted pilgrims from around the world especially from southern India. A recently launched ferry service between the port and southern India brings back to life, historical and cultural connections.

Hot Springs In Keerimalai (21)

Keerimalai Hot Springs is a natural freshwater spring located on the coast opposite the Keerimalai Naguleswaram Kovil. A bathing pool is built around the underground spring and separated from the sea by a stone wall. Visitors flock to Keerimalai to take a dip at this idyllic spot. Enriched with minerals, these healing waters are famed for their miraculous therapeutic and curative properties.

Keerimalai Naguleswaram Kovil (22)

One of the oldest shrines on the Island and the most northernmost is the Keerimalai Naguleswaram Kovil.

Prior to the arrival of Prince Vijaya (the legendary forefather of the Sinhalese) to Lanka, the island was inhabited by two tribes; the "Yakkhas" and "Nagas". They practiced an early form of Hinduism worshipping Lord Shiva.

There are five recognised ancient abodes (Pancha Iswarams) of Shiva spread out over the island's coasts. Mythology proclaims that these five temples were built by Ravana, King of Lanka and devout follower of the god Shiva.

Naguleswaram, historically known also as the Thirutambaleswaram Kovil, is the northernmost of five hallowed Lord Shiva temples, the others are Ketheeswaram temple, Koneswaram Temple, Munneswaram temple and Tondeswaram temple, all venerated by Hindus from around the world.

Kathurugoda Viharaya, Kantharodai (23)

Near the area of Chunnakam around 12 miles (19 km) north of Jaffna is the Kathurugoda Viharaya at Kantharodai.

It is believed that this religious site was established in the 3rd century BC during the reign of King Devanampiya Tissa (250-210 BC) who was credited with the implementation of Buddhism on the Island.

Kathurugoda Viharaya contains the ruins of around 60 miniature dagobas, said to be over 2,000 years old. The stupas are made of grey coloured coral stone, the largest stupa being 23 ft (7 m) in diameter.

Some believe that the dagobas enshrine the remains of 80 Buddhist monks who died of food poisoning, others believe that they are votive in nature. Various artefacts that were discovered at this archaeological site, including Bodhisattva sculptures, a guard stone and coins, are on display at Jaffna's Archaeological Museum.

Dambakola Patuna Sanghamitta Temple (24)

Situated 12 miles (19 km) north of Jaffna Town is the ancient port of Dambakola Patuna.

On the December full-moon, around 240 BC, the daughter of Indian Emperor Asoka, Princess Sanghamitta (sister of Mahinda, who introduced Buddhism to Sri Lanka), stepped onto the shores of Lanka. She was carrying a sapling from the original Bo Tree beneath which the Buddha attained Supreme Enlightenment in Bodhgaya, India, in 483 BC.

Princess Sanghamitta was received by King Devanampiya Tissa (250-210 BC) and the sapling was carried in great procession and planted in Anuradhapura.

The Bo Tree continues to flourish to this day and is the most sacred place of Buddhist worship known as Sri Maha Bodhi.

King Tissa built a temple at the port to commemorate the arrival of the Princess with the sapling.

Jaffna - The Islands

Towards the west of Jaffna, a string of islands scatter into the waters of the Palk Bay towards India.

One of the joys of visiting Jaffna is accessing and exploring these delightful islands that time has forgotten. Getting to them is an adventure in itself and undoubtedly a trip where you can discover some hidden treasures.

The islands Karainagar, Kayts, and Punkudutivu are all connected to the mainland by causeways.

Karainagar

Eluvaitivu

Analaitivu

Kayt

Nagadeepa

Palk Bay

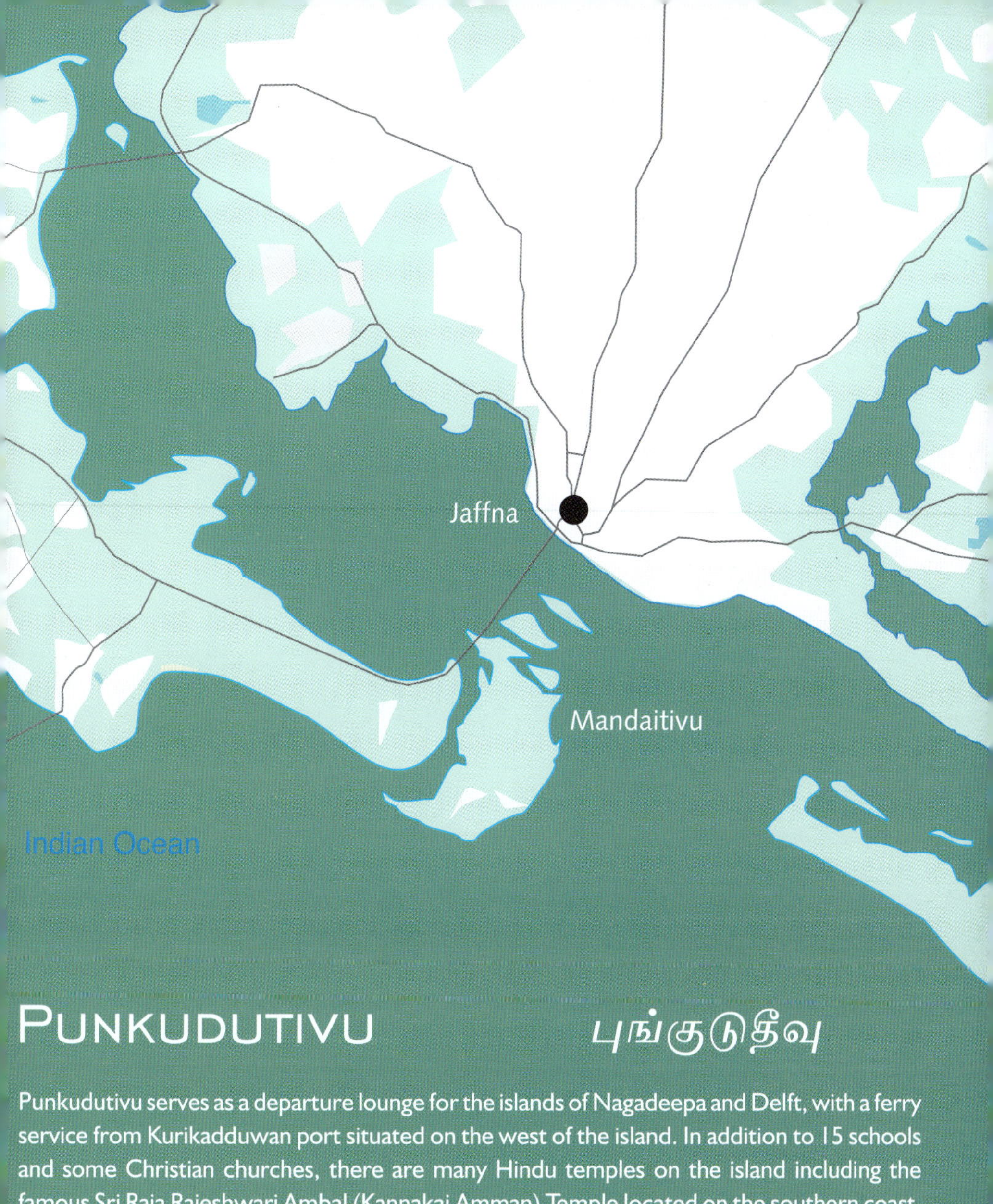

Jaffna

Mandaitivu

Indian Ocean

PUNKUDUTIVU புங்குடுதீவு

Punkudutivu serves as a departure lounge for the islands of Nagadeepa and Delft, with a ferry service from Kurikadduwan port situated on the west of the island. In addition to 15 schools and some Christian churches, there are many Hindu temples on the island including the famous Sri Raja Rajeshwari Ambal (Kannakai Amman) Temple located on the southern coast. The lighthouse east of the temple is an unusual square shape tower about 25 ft (7.5 m) tall.

Karainagar Island

காரைநகர்

1. CASUARINA BEACH
2. SIVAN TEMPLE
3. KOVALAM LIGHTHOUSE
4. KOVALAM BEACH

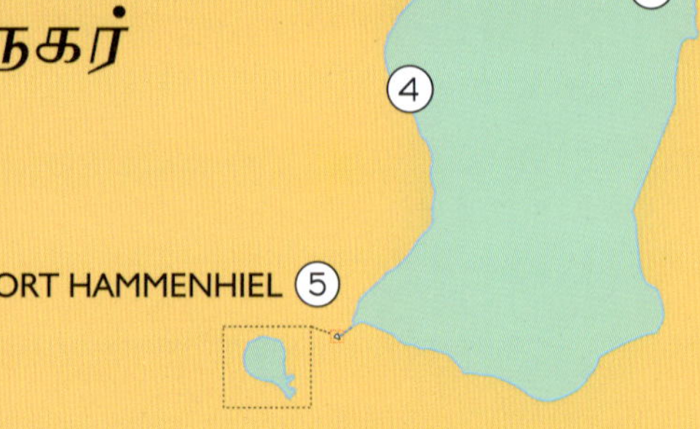

Karainagar Island, also known as Karaitivu, is connected to the mainland by the Karainagar causeway Bridge. Karainagar (named after its Karai trees) is about 8.5 sq miles (22 sq km) with about 11,000 inhabitants. A third of its land is used for paddy cultivation.

Casuarina Beach (1)

Along the northern perimeter is Casuarina Beach, named after the Casuarina trees that fringe its shore. Early morning, fishermen can be seen dragging out their boats going fishing and evenings offer a good view of the sunset.

Sivan Temple (2)

South of Casuarina Beach is Karainagar Sivan Temple, dedicated to Lord Shiva.

Kovalam Lighthouse (3)

West of Casuarina Beach is the Kovalam Lighthouse. Built in 1916 by the British it is about 82 ft (25 m) in height.

Kovalam Beach (4)

Travelling south of Kovalam Lighthouse is Kovalam Beach, an isolated beach perfect at sunset.

FORT HAMMENHIEL (5)

Fort Hammenhiel is situated on a small piece of land just off Karainagar Island's south eastern tip, and a short ferry ride will get you there.

Built by the Portuguese in mid-17th century and named Fortaleza Real (Fort Royal), it guarded the western entrance to Jaffna lagoon. The Dutch captured the fort in 1658 and renamed it Hammenhiel (Heel of the Ham). After rebuilding the fort, it housed about 30 soldiers. When the British took over the fort, they used it as a prison and a hospital for the treatment of infectious diseases.

Kayts Island

ஊர்காவற்துறை

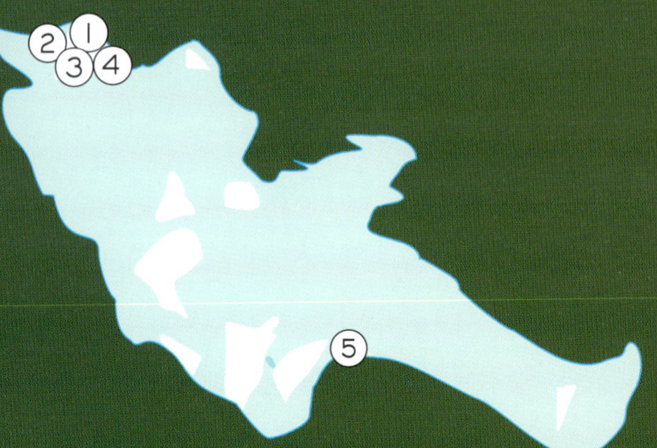

1. KAYTS HARBOUR
2. KAYTS ISLAND FORT
3. SIVAN KOVIL
4. ST. ANTHONY'S CHURCH
5. CHADDY BEACH

Kayts is the largest of the islands on the peninsula connected to the mainland by a causeway. The size of the island is about 25 sq miles (65 sq km) with a population around 27,000. There are plenty of temples, churches and mosques to visit.

Kayts Harbour (1)

This is an ancient port called Uruthota where Indian merchant ships traded and elephants were exported to India. As with Galle, it is believed that this port was also visited by King Solomon's merchant vessels.

Kayts Island Fort (2)

Constructed by the Portuguese in the north of the island in 1629 and named Urundi, this horseshoe shaped fort close to the port had two bastions and housed 40 soldiers.

After the expulsion of the Portuguese, it was taken over by the Dutch.

Sivan Kovil (3)

Dedicated to Shiva this shrine was constructed during the Chola dynasty between 993 – 1077.

With its numerous festivals celebrated throughout the year it is a very popular temple among locals, and it is an important pilgrimage site for devotees from all over the island.

St. Anthony's Church (4)

The origin of St. Anthony's goes back to 1820 and it is one of the oldest churches in Jaffna. Having undergone extensive renovations, the church celebrated its bicentenary in 2020.

Chaddy Beach (5)

Located south of the island is a tranquil endless white sand beach with crystal clear water and plenty of shade. Popular with the locals.

Kurikadduwan Jetty

NAGADEEPA

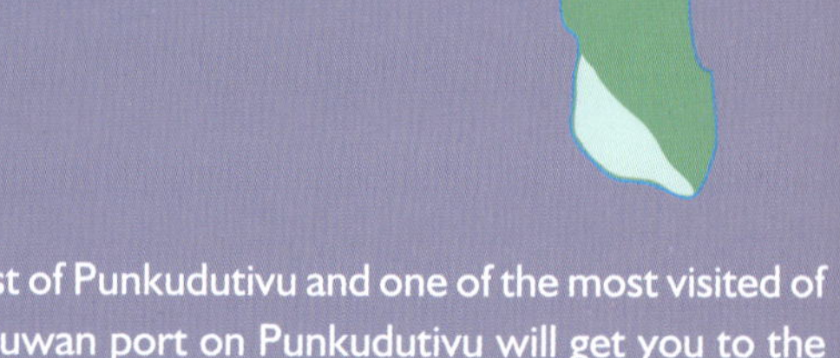

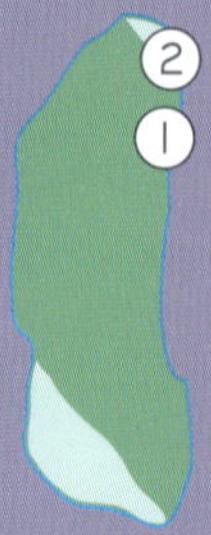

1. NAGADEEPA PURANA VIHARAYA
2. NAGAPOOSHANI AMMAN KOVIL

Nagadeepa is a small but important island west of Punkudutivu and one of the most visited of the islands. A short ferry ride from Kurikadduwan port on Punkudutivu will get you to the island, also known as Nainativu, an ancient site steeped in history with major spiritual significance.

NAGADEEPA PURANA VIHARAYA (1)

For Buddhists the temple Nagadeepa Purana Viharaya is one of Sri Lanka's holiest of shrines where Lord Buddha Himself is said to have visited, the stupa having been built at the site where Lord Buddha preached His Dhamma to the Naga clans. Every year, during the full moon in the month of April, many devotees from around the country make a pilgrimage to this shrine as they have done continually since the 1st century.

Nagapooshani Amman Kovil (2)

நயினாதீவு நாகபூசணி அம்மன் கோயில்

The Nagapooshani Amman Kovil is famed for being one of the oldest Hindu kovils in Sri Lanka.

This ancient kovil is dedicated to the Hindu deity Nagapooshani Amman in connection with the Naga tribes who lived on the island.

During the month of Aani (June / July), this ornate and colourful temple is the focus of a 16-day Mahostavam festival, where more than 100,000 devotees attend from all over Sri Lanka.

IMUL-A 0045 CHW

Delft Island

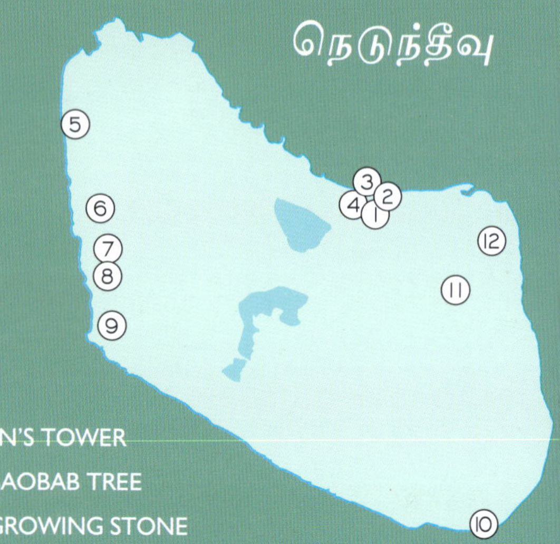

1. OLD DUTCH HOSPITAL
2. PIGEON NEST
3. DELFT BEACH
4. DUTCH FORT
5. VEDIYARASAN FORT
6. SIVAN KOVIL
7. GIANTS FOOTPRINT
8. HORSE STABLES
9. HORSE SIGHTINGS
10. QUEEN'S TOWER
11. THE BAOBAB TREE
12. THE GROWING STONE

The remotest inhabited island west of the mainland is Delft Island. Covering an area of 17 sq miles (44 sq km), this flat, semi-arid, windswept coral island with tall Palmyra trees, has a population of around 4,100 people. An hour on the ferry will bring you from Kurikadduwan port Punkudutivu to this unique tropical island encircled with shallow water and beautiful beaches.

Hiring a jeep on arrival is the best way to get around these rugged roads lined with houses and walls uniquely made of coral and limestone with plaited Palmyra leaf thatched roofs.

Delft has a rich heritage from the Chola dynasty, the Portuguese, the Dutch (who gave the island its name), to the British. Around 7 sq miles (18 sq km) of the island has been designated a National Park.

Old Dutch Hospital (1)

West of the jetty is the Dutch Hospital built in the 17th century by the Dutch East India company and used for 200 years. This long single-story building with a wide veranda, made using limestone and corals, is a good example of Dutch colonial architecture. As well as the large rooms for patients the hospital also has a small chapel where religious services were held for patients and staff. The Dutch Hospital was used as an administrative centre during the British rule. Sympathetically restored it now serves as a museum housing artefacts from the Dutch colonial period.

Pigeon Nest (2)

Behind the Dutch Hospital is an ancient pigeon's nest (dovecote).

The Dutch kept homing pigeons and used them to carry messages between Delft Island and Jaffna.

The use of the messenger pigeons continued during the British colonial era.

Delft Beach (3)

Delft island is surrounded by beautiful sandy beaches and turquoise blue waters. Delft Beach is charming and serene with calm seas during the southwest monsoon. Sharp coral fringe most of the island, making some beaches unsuitable for swimming.

With a bit of exploring, it is possible to find your own idyllic stretch of beach to enjoy.

DUTCH FORT (4)

Made with coral and limestone the fort was built by the Portuguese to protect the Jaffna Peninsula. Only ruins of the larger walls of its unique shape remain.

It was later taken over by the Dutch who built a barrack nearby.

VEDIYARASAN FORT (5)

Ancient Buddhist chronicles inform us that all the islands adjacent to Jaffna were inhabited by Buddhist Monks and a number of Buddhist temples were sited on Delft Island during the Anuradhapura period. This site has seen human inhabitants since the 2nd century BC.

The remains of three ancient stupas were discovered on the north-western coast at Vediyarasan Fort as well as other relics including fragments of Buddha statues. Uniquely for Sri Lankan monastic architecture, the stupas, of varying sizes, are built of coral. The base of the main stupa, placed on an elevated platform measures 34 ft (10 m) in diameter.

An inscription written in Brahmi script found with the stupas dates the site back to 1st or 2nd century AD.

Local folklore states that before delivering the sapling of the Sacred Bo Tree to King Tissa at port of Dambakola Patuna, Jaffna, Princess Sanghamitta took rest at this very place on the island.

SIVAN KOVIL (6)

South of Vediyarasan Fort are the ruins of an ancient Hindu shrine. Sivan Kovil was built around the 11th century and constructed in the medieval Dravidian style. Only the Antaralaya (foyer) and the sanctum remain.

Many coins of the same period were also discovered at this site.

Giants Footprint (7)

Located west of the island engraved on the stone surface is the Giants Footprint.

The local Hindus believe that the footprint is that of Hanuman the magical deity who led the monkey army to help Rama rescue his wife, Sita, from the evil king Ravana of Lanka.

Horse Stables (8)

A few hundred meters behind the Giants Footprint are the ruins of the horse stables. During the British colonial period, the Irishman Lieutenant Nolan, an officer in the engineer corps of the 4th Ceylon Regiment was appointed administrator of Delft in 1811. Lieutenant Nolan's original mission was to develop the growing of flax on the island, however he was also given the charge of horse-breeding on Delft Island. Nolan built three large stables, for the training of untamed horses; he also imported and introduced a new bloodline to the existing livestock. The stables are an archaeologically protected monument.

Delft Island

Horse Sightings (9)

On the dry grassland littered with bleached coral, freely roam a colony of wild horses. The Portuguese introduced horses, brought from Arabia, to the island in the 16th century to use as workhorses for the army. These animals were also bred on the island and traded with the Indian subcontinent. Often referred to as ponies, due to their size, their ancestors were huge Arabian horses, but have shrunk from generation to generation.

Estimated at about 500 in number, these horses are iconic and are protected. There are also an estimated 10,000 cows on the island roaming freely on the grassland and a really important part of the island's economy, with ghee being its main export.

Queens Tower (10)

Located on the southern tip of the island is the Queen's Tower, also known as Quindah Tower. Built by the British, at a height of 55 ft (17 m) this square limestone tower with five stories, tapers towards the top.

The exact purpose of its use has not been agreed upon. With a central flue, it may have served as a lighthouse where a fire was lit at its base causing smoke to be emitted through the stack serving as a warning to maritime seafarers. However, the most popular theory is that it was built as a trigonometric point and twinned with the King's Tower (remains of which are on the northern tip) worked as a triangulation station.

The Baobab Tree (11)

The baobab tree is native to the African savannah, Madagascar and North-western Australia where the climate is dry and arid. It is believed that the baobab tree, located south of the jetty, was brought to the island by Arab traders and planted during the Portuguese era. Also known as the Elephant tree (as its bark resembles elephant skin), it stores water in the trunk to endure harsh drought climatic conditions. The tree produces large aromatic flowers and is an archaeologically protected monument.

Growing Stone (12)

The most unusual sight on the island is the sacred growing stone, venerated by the locals. They fervently believe that this rock, now 5 ft (1.5 m) tall, has been growing over the years.

Wrapped in a shimmering cloth, it appears to be taking the shape of a cobra.

N 08° 51' 18"
E 80° 12' 10"

Our Lady of Madhu

With a history dating over 400 years, Our Lady of Madhu in the Mannar Diocese, is the holiest Roman Catholic Church on the island, visited by pilgrims not only of the Christian faith but by Buddhists and Hindus as well.

Since their arrival on the island in 1505 the Portuguese were vociferously converting the native Islanders to Catholicism, and in their zeal for evangelisation ruthlessly destroyed Buddhist and Hindu Temples. The Dutch were more tolerant towards the natives when they gained control of the Island in 1656. However, they too started to spread their form of Christianity, the Dutch Reformed Church. The subsequent persecution of the Catholics by the Dutch and the Jaffna King forced 20 Catholic families to flee from the northeast coast of Manthai along with a statue of The Virgin Mary to the safer location of Madhu. They were later joined by another 700 Catholics fleeing from Jaffna. Madhu was the perfect location for the community, installing their statue in a new shrine, and this small church gradually earned a reputation for possessing the power of healing attracting even more devotees.

In 1687 Father Joseph Vaz came to Ceylon from Goa to save and restore the Catholic Church on the Island. In 1705 he renovated and expanded the small shrine of Our Lady of Madhu. In 1868, the arrival of Oblate Bishop Christopher Bonjean saw more extensive renovations, and in 1872 the famous annual pilgrimage was initiated. Every August, the tranquil town of Madhu witnesses the arrival of hundreds of thousands of Roman Catholics from all parts of Sri Lanka to celebrate the annual feast of the Visitation.

In honour of the profound religious, spiritual and divine nature of the shrine, in 1924 Pope Pius XI granted the image of Our Lady of Madhu a Canonical Coronation. In June 1995, Father Joseph Vaz was beatified in Sri Lanka by Pope John Paul II, and later in 2015 was canonized by Pope Francis I at Galle Face Green.

Tantirimale Raja Maha Vihara

N 08° 32' 00"
E 80° 16' 00"

Located about 25 miles (40 km) northwest of Anuradhapura on the border of Wilpattu National Park is the sacred monastic complex of Tantirimale which dates back to the reign of King Devanampiya Tissa (250-210 BC).

Ancient chronicles state that in 240 BC, Princess Sanghamitta, who brought to Sri Lanka a sapling from the original Bo Tree beneath which the Buddha attained supreme Enlightenment in Bodhgaya, India, rested the night at Tantirimale on her way to Anuradhapura. A branch of the sapling was later planted at the temple and to this day, it is the most sanctified object of veneration by thousands of pilgrims.

The monastery is centred around a beautiful Dagoba, and is set amid a rocky landscape surrounded by the lush jungle with natural ponds full of lotus flowers, which served as bathing ponds for the reclusive monks that lived in the nearby caves. Some of the caverns have evidence of an ancient civilisation with murals of tigers, deer and of heavenly bodies such as sun and moon dating over 4,000 years drawn by aboriginal inhabitants of the island.

The main Buddha statue at Tantirimale is about 8 ft (2.4 m) in height and is in a Samadhi or meditation posture. The Buddha statue in the recumbent posture is about 40 ft (12 m) long. Both these statues, hewn from the rock, have similarities with the Gal Vihara images in Polonnaruwa. The monastery flourished from the latter part of the Anuradhapura period onwards, and during the Polonnaruwa period, this beautiful, tranquil and serene monastery of Tantirimale was one of the most important shrines of worship.

Elite
GUIDE
Jungle Monastery

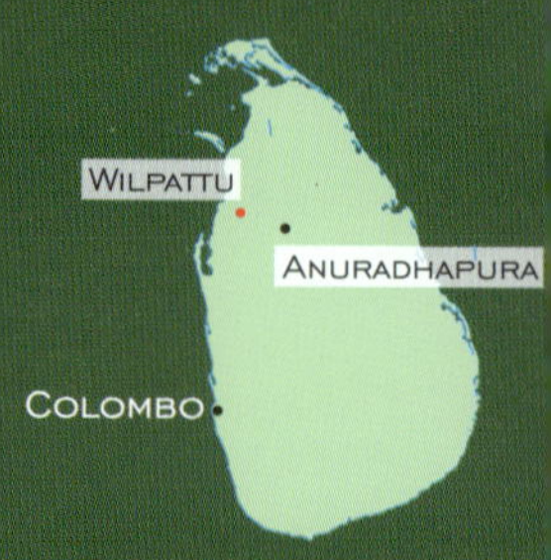

WILPATTU NATIONAL PARK

N 08° 26' 00"
E 80° 00' 00"

විල්පත්තු ජාතික වනෝද්‍යානය

Situated on the west coast about 25 miles (40 km) from Anuradhapura is the oldest and largest National Park on the island.

It is believed that these copper-coloured shores were the actual landing site of Prince Vijaya, the legendary forefather of the Sinhalese, and his followers in 483 BC. Prince Vijaya married Princess Kuveni of the Yakka tribe, and her palace has been identified as the ancient ruins at Kali Villu within the National Park.

At Pomparippu there is an ancient burial site with about 8,000 burial urns containing the remains of over 10,000 people from pre-Vijayan times.

Wilpattu, with its open grassy plains, wetlands, and dense scrub jungle, has an abundance of wildlife with a reputation as the best place for spotting leopards. Other major attractions include the Asian Elephant, Sloth Bear, Spotted Deer, Asiatic Buffalo, Grey Slender Loris, Mugger Crocodile and over 150 species of birds. The best time to view these animals is either on an early morning safari or at dusk.

Elite
GUIDE

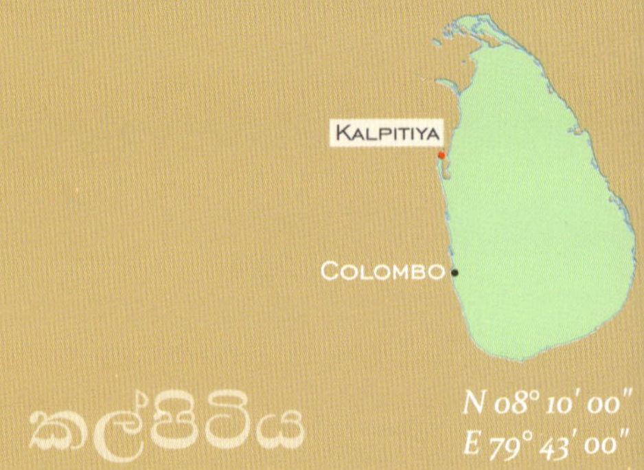

කල්පිටිය

N 08° 10' 00"
E 79° 43' 00"

KALPITIYA PENINSULA

About 105 miles (170 km) north of Colombo on Sri Lanka's west coast lies the remote Kalpitiya peninsula, an area rich in natural diversity known for its serene beaches along with a sandbank, lagoon and 14 islands.

Kalpitiya is a simple fishing village where the pristine azure waters of the Indian Ocean are ideal for swimming and other activities, including wind-surfing, kayaking, snorkelling and scuba diving. However, what attracts enthusiasts from all over the world to this unspoilt beautiful stretch of sand is that this is one of the best kitesurfing destinations in Asia.

With kitesurfing possible all year round, Kalpitiya has several kite schools for beginners and professionals alike. The main seasons for this sport are from May to September when the winds are quite strong, and from December to March when the winds are lighter.

Boat excursions from Alankuda beach can take you not far from the shore, where you can see dolphins in their hundreds swimming alongside. Kalpitiya is also a feeding ground for migrating Blue and Sperm Whales, especially from December to April when they can be seen rising from the depths to breathe.

A boat ride or canoe trip on the lagoon brings you closer to nature with its rich biodiversity, home to several species of migratory birds. Additionally, there is the unique experience of camping on one of the remote islands.

Go Fly A Kite

Elite
GUIDE

The Viceroy Special

The Viceroy is the only passenger steam train operational in Sri Lanka. British-built, this locomotive was named after its appearance in the film Mountbatten The Last Viceroy. This luxury train has two air-conditioned observation cars furnished in period style, each with 32 plush reclining seats and individual tables. Each saloon has an adjoining smokers' lounge. The restaurant and bar carriage is decorated with Edwardian ribbed fans and teak-trimmed panelling. Here, snacks and three-course meals are skilfully prepared by first class chefs, and served by liveried stewards throughout your journey.

There is no better way to view the most stunning mountain scenery of the hill country or beautiful palm-fringed beaches of the west coast. This graceful and romantic journey through time evokes memories of the British Raj.

Trips vary between day excursions and all-inclusive package tours. A popular journey is Colombo to Rambukkana near Kandy, where you can disembark to visit the Pinnawala Elephant Orphanage.

Steam Locomotive

Mount Lavinia

ගල්කිස්ස

The Mount Lavinia is Sri Lanka's most beautiful hotel with undoubtably the friendliest of staff. Cocktails at sunset on the terrace followed by dinner is a truly awesome experience.

N 06° 49' 59"
E 79° 51' 43"

Mount Lavinia, located 8 miles (13 km) south of Colombo, was formerly a fishing village known as Galkissa. A side road heading away from the busy Galle Road leads to the elegance and tranquillity of the old colonial hotel, The Mount Lavinia, from which the area gets its name.

Built in 1806 as the country residence for the British Governor, Thomas Maitland, it is situated on a promontory of land with spectacular views of the coast and Colombo. Legend has it that Governor Maitland was so captivated by Lovina, a beautiful and talented dancer from a low caste, who performed for him in his stately residence, that a romance soon ensued. Away from the disapproving eyes of the British society in Colombo, the aristocratic Governor would smuggle his lover through an underground tunnel leading into his house, and so their secret liaisons continued.

Today, a magnificent ballroom adjoins the old house, with the hotel set along a superb beach. Newly-weds from all over the world honeymoon at the island's most romantic residence which offers modern facilities whilst exuding colonial charm. Thomas Maitland's secret tunnel remains to this day, and serves as a reminder of Mount Lavinia's early amorous days!

Elite
GUIDE

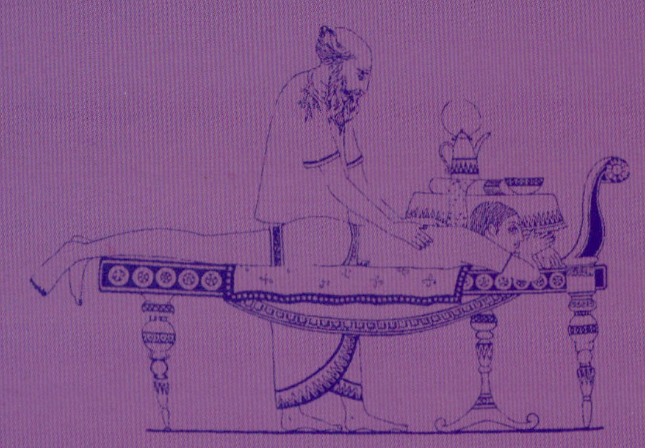

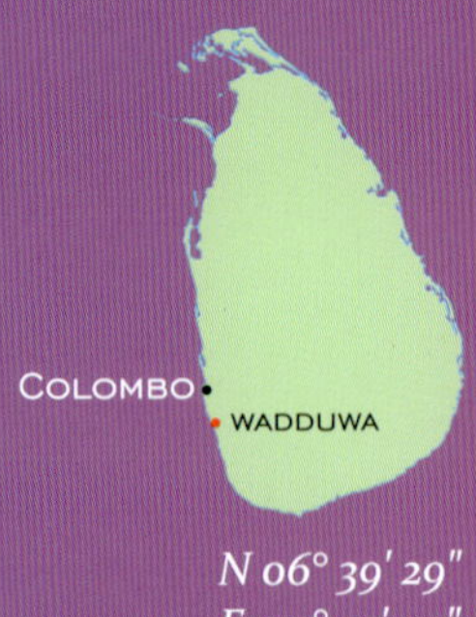

ආයුර්වේද

AYURVEDA

Ayurveda is the world's oldest holistic health care system, and is considered a prerequisite for human well-being. Many visitors to Sri Lanka come specifically to experience this ancient cultural healing practice, using the island's prolific herb and plant life to cure and revitalise.

Herbal medication and massage, sauna, oil treatment and yoga are all part of the detoxifying, stress-relieving and rejuvenating programme.

The most established and authentic experience can be found at the Siddhalepa Ayurveda Health Resort in Wadduwa. This beautiful, unique haven with its own beach is dedicated to the nurturing of body, mind and spirit.

The therapies are specifically designed for each individual and administered by a team of eminent Ayurveda scholars who descend from four generations of Ayurvedic knowledge.

All medicinal oils and tonics are manufactured in-house to international standards. The resort specialises in pure Ayurvedic food, carefully prepared under guidance of the doctors.

A short stay at the sanctuary will rebalance, revitalise and re-invigorate you for many months.
Siddhalepa Ayurveda Health Resort   www.siddhalepa.com

Healing

N 06° 41' 25"
E 80° 22' 48"

RATNAPURA

About 60 miles (100 km) south-east of Colombo lies the town of Ratnapura, the "city of gems".

Climatically one of the wettest towns in Sri Lanka, Ratnapura is the gem mining centre of Sri Lanka where ancient traditional methods of mining are still in use today. Gem mining is a co-operative effort, and when gems are discovered, profits are shared between its members.

Visitors can browse the many workshops to observe the hand polishing of stones. The most popular gem found in Sri Lanka is the blue sapphire.

Other gems mined include ruby, topaz, amethyst, cat's eye, alexandrite, aquamarine, tourmaline, garnet and zircon.

King Solomon gave a great ruby to the Queen of Sheba, which is thought to have been mined at Ratnapura. The British crown jewels contain a 400-carat blue sapphire known as "Blue Belle" which is also accredited to Sri Lanka.

This area also provides evidence of early cultures and extinct wildlife.

Adam's Peak

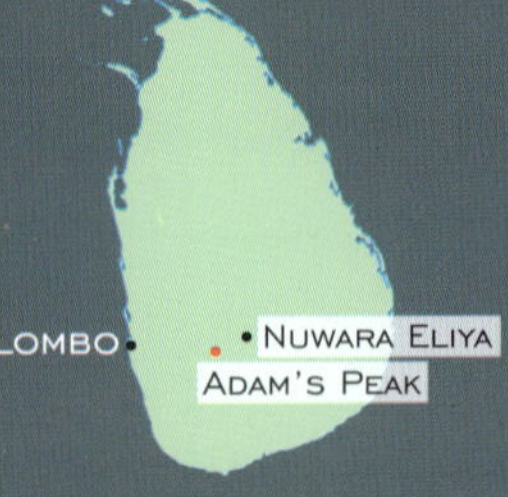

ශ්‍රීපාදය

N 06° 48′ 43″
E 80° 29′ 58″

Adam's Peak is the fifth highest mountain in Sri Lanka. At 7,360 ft (2,243 m) it is located within the 60,000 acre (24,300 hectare) Peak Wilderness Sanctuary.

The ancient name for the mountain was Samanala kanda, "The mountain of Saman", after the god Saman, one of the four guardian deities who watches over the island. The Sinhala name for the mountain is Sri Pada, "Holy Footprint".

The Mahavamsa made reference to Lord Buddha's footprint left on top of this mountain, and since the 11th century AD, Sri Pada has attracted countless numbers of visitors to worship it. King Vijayabahu I (1055-1110) and King Nissanka Malla (1187-1196) both recorded their pilgrimages to the mountain.

Shadow

All four major religions of Sri Lanka venerate Sri Pada as their holy mountain. The Buddhists strongly believe that the footprint on this mountain was left by the Lord Buddha on one of His visits to the island. The Hindus accredit the footprint to Lord Shiva; the Christians say it is that of St. Thomas ("Doubting Thomas") who became a missionary to the East. The Muslims claim that it was Adam's footprint, imprinted when he left heaven and first set foot in the Garden of Eden, Sri Lanka. Whatever one's beliefs, no other location is so venerated by all religions.

The ideal time to climb Adam's Peak is from December to May, when the weather is calmer. The climbing season peaks in March, and tens of thousands of people make the ascent each year.

There are two routes to the top. The one from Ratnapura is the longer route: 16 miles (26 km) by foot, or 9 miles (14 km) by vehicle and then 7 miles (11 km) by foot and certainly the most arduous. The other route from Maskeliya begins at a higher elevation and is a considerably shorter ascent of 4.5 miles (7 km).

We would recommend the shorter route from Maskeliya. It should take around 4 hours, including rest breaks, to reach the summit. However long it takes, remember it is not a race, so take your time and enjoy the journey along the way as well as the final destination.

During Buddha's missionary labours, He visited the ancient island of Lanka on three separate occasions. His first descent was in the central plains at Mahiyangana, where a dagoba has been constructed in honour of this event.

His second visit was to Nagadeepa in the north of the island. His third and final visit was to Kelaniya, close to Colombo. When Lord Buddha gravitated home, He passed over the central mountains and His foot touched Samanala kanda (now known as Sri Pada or "Adam's Peak"), leaving an imprint there.

It is important to climb late at night, when it is cooler, and aim to get to the summit just before sunrise at around 6am. Arriving at the top too early will mean that you will have to wait in typically windy and very cold conditions.

Stalls selling beverages and savoury snacks are stationed at regular intervals along the route of the climb. These are good places to stop and rest with a cup of hot sweet tea to boost your energy levels, but give the food a miss – take your own supplies instead. Interestingly, the tea gets more expensive the higher up the mountain you climb! At one pilgrim's rest, the Siddhalepa Ayurveda station, you can have your feet and neck massaged with Ayurvedic oils, courtesy of Siddhalepa. This is a welcome pit stop for many a weary hiker.

The path and the stairways are well lit. A trail of lights stretches away, on and upwards, to the point where they blend into the stars, so whilst climbing, it is impossible to know the exact location of the summit.

On the way up, you will pass people descending. If you ask them how far it is to the top, you will invariably get the reply, "Not far now"!

At another pilgrim's rest nearer the summit, you will see masses of threads woven along the railings. This ritual is performed by the devout who believe that it was here that Lord Buddha paused to mend His robes.

During the climb, the continual ringing of the pilgrims' bell can be heard, increasing in volume the higher you climb. Recent ascendants to the summit ring the bell to signify the number of their completed pilgrimages. (The current journey is not included, as it is not completed until you descend safely).

The summit can be quite busy, especially close to sunrise. A small temple is built over the giant footprint, which is actually covered by a huge stone slab on which a replica is carved. Also located on the summit are quarters for monks and a post box.

On a clear day the dawn is quite spectacular, but you will need a bit of luck regarding the weather. As the day dawns, the hill country rises to the east, while the west slopes to the sea. As the sun ascends, it casts a shadow of the mountain over the land. This is a fantastic phenomenon, a perfect triangle, which reaches its maximum and then dips a little before rising and disappearing. It is said that the dipping of the shadow is due to the sun bowing his head in reverence to Adam's Peak.

Descending Adam's Peak is in some ways more difficult, as it is then that you realise that the height of the steps varies greatly, so you will need to take care as you make your way down. It may take you a good few hours to descend, but it will probably take a good few days to recover!

Advice

- Use the route from Maskeliya.
- Wear comfortable shoes for the climb.
- Although the weather will be warm at the base, it can be extremely cold on the summit, so carry some extra clothing since you may have to wait for sunrise.
- Time your climb to start around 1am, which will give you 5 hours to get to the top.
- Drink hot, sweet tea en route and avoid food from the vendors (toilets are few and very basic).
- Full moon days (Poya) will be extremely busy, so are best avoided.
- Keep going, you will get there!

සිංහරාජ වනාන්තරය

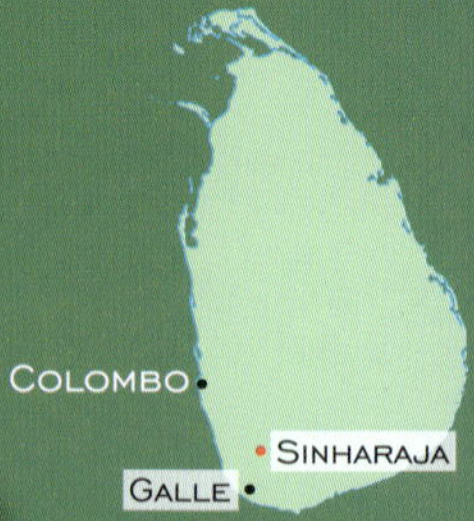

Sinharaja Rainforest

Russell's Viper

Colombo
Sinharaja
Galle

N 06° 25' 16"
E 80° 23' 18"

The Sinharaja rainforest lies in the south-west lowland wet zone between Ratnapura and the south coast. It is the oldest remaining primeval tropical rainforest on the island. Declared a biosphere reserve in April 1978, it was inscribed on UNESCO's World Heritage List in 1988.

Climatically, Sinharaja rainforest has an average annual rainfall of 140 to 200 inches (3,600 mm to 5,000 mm). The majority of this rainfall occurs during the south-west monsoons between May and July and the north-east monsoons between November and January. Temperatures range from 66°-93°F (19°-34°C).

Sinharaja, which means "lion king", has been left undisturbed to evolve and is thus one of the most important areas in Sri Lanka, as well as being internationally recognised for its bio-diversity. More than 60 per cent of the trees are endemic and many of them are considered rare. Also considered rare are a number of insects and amphibians.

The forest is particularly known for its birds, of which 21 are endemic species, including the Scops owl and the red faced Malkoha.

There are also over 20 species of snake; more than half are endemic, including the arboreal green pit viper. In addition, the forest is home to the endemic purple-faced langur, the endemic golden palm civet, a giant squirrel and the fishing cat.

The leopard is the top carnivore in Sinharaja, but is rarely seen due to the dense nature of the forest; however a black leopard was sighted in 2001.

Sinharaja is the only rainforest in Sri Lanka that is promoted to nature lovers and trekkers, but it is protected from over visitation. One entrance to the forest is located on the south-eastern side, near Deniyaya. A good place to stay in Deniyaya is at Sinharaja Rest. The proprietor, Palitha Ratnayaka and his brother Bandula, organise treks through the forest (around 3 miles [5 km] each way) to a beautiful waterfall and natural pool for a swim. Palitha adores his forest and enjoys leading groups of visitors at a pace suitable for all. He is extremely knowledgeable about the variety of indigenous flora and fauna and there is nothing about the forest he doesn't know! Rooms at the Sinharaja Rest are very basic, but the food is great and Palitha makes everyone feel very much at home. Treks start early, around 8:30am, when the jeeps leave for the forest entrance. It is advisable to book the guesthouse and the trek in advance.

Sinharaja Rest
Temple Road
Deniyaya
Tel 041 227 3367

Calotes calotes
Green Garden Lizard

Bentota

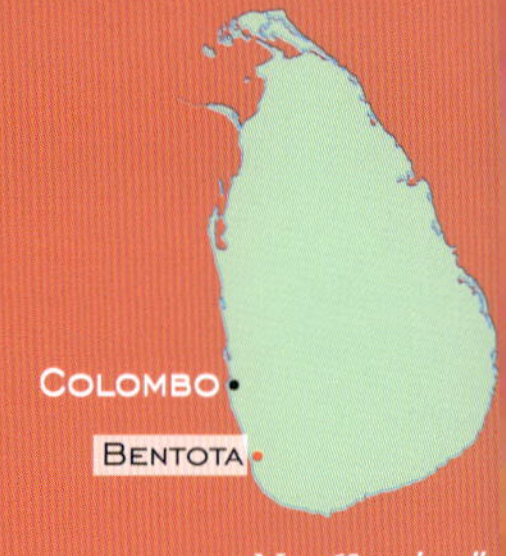

N 06° 25' 15"
E 79° 59' 54"

Bentota is a popular tourist resort, with great beaches spread along quiet seas, excellent hotels, restaurants, market places and souvenir shops.

Located 35 miles (56 km) south of Colombo, Bentota was used as a stop off point on the way to Galle, where the Rest House (now Bentota Beach Hotel) provided sustenance for travellers.

Sports lovers are well catered for here, and, because of the long lagoon and calm seas from November to April, it is ideal for water sports including sailing, wind surfing, water skiing and jet skiing.

For the less energetic, deep-sea fishing, or perhaps a relaxing river safari up the Bentota Ganga to see the bird life and crocodiles may be more appropriate.

Bentota is also rapidly gaining a reputation for ayurvedic treatments because of the development of healing centres.

About 10 miles (16 km) inland at Kalawila is the "Brief Garden". This paradise garden was the lifelong passion of the late Bevis Bawa, the celebrated landscape architect, writer and sculptor. The garden has an enchanting array of exotic plants, trees and water features, set on a hillside yielding superb views. Bawa's collection of furniture, photographs, paintings and sculptures are also impressive.

Hikkaduwa

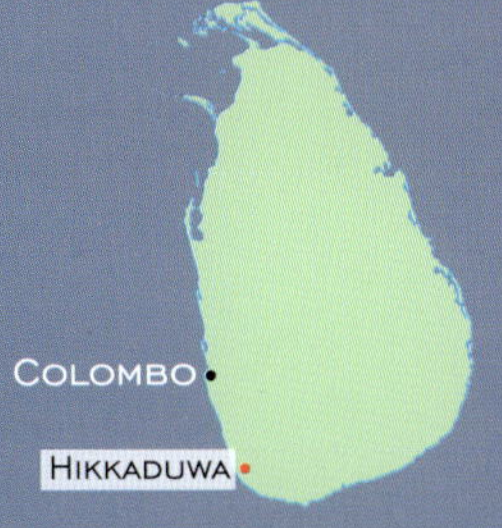

N 06° 08′ 32″
E 80° 06′ 01″

Around 20 miles (32 km) south of Bentota and 55 miles (88 km) from Colombo is the charming little fishing village of Hikkaduwa, which has been a favourite bathing spot since the 1930s.

Popularised by young travellers in the 1960s, Hikkaduwa is now a very busy tourist resort a couple of miles long, with bars, fast food and discotheques that all come alive after dark.

Hikkaduwa's main attraction is the colourful coral reef situated a short distance from the shore, populated with exotic fish and turtles. A sanctuary has been designated between the shore and the reef in order to protect it. The waters over the reef are about 10-13 ft (3-4 m) deep, and the best way they can be observed is by snorkelling or, for the less sporting, through a glass-bottomed boat for hire in several places along the beach.

There are many scuba-diving stations licensed to teach PADI courses, so divers can explore the many fascinating shipwrecks around the area.

South of Hikkaduwa, the impressive waves attract international surfers and surfboards can be hired locally. Although the sea in this area offers good swimming and snorkelling, be aware that the currents can be strong.

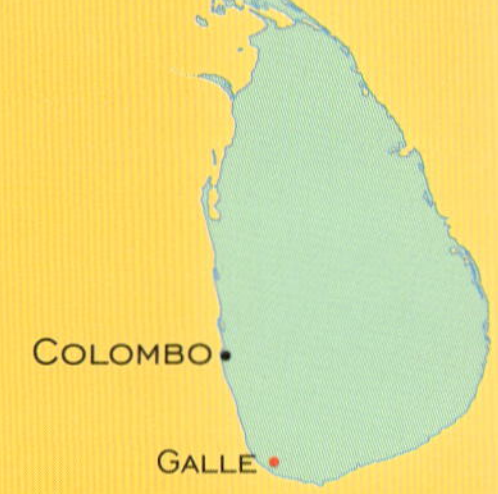

GALLE

N 06° 01' 39"
E 80° 13' 01"

ගාල්ල

It is widely believed that Galle may have been the city of Tarshish of Biblical times, the great emporium of the East, trading with Chinese, Persian, Indian and Arab traders and where King Solomon sent merchant vessels to buy gold, silver, gems, ivory and spices.

A Portuguese fleet first landed in Galle in 1505 after taking shelter in the harbour when their ship was blown off course. Gradually, they developed trading links with the island. In 1589 they built a small fort in Galle to guard the harbour and named it Santa Cruz.

Dutch Fort

The Dutch arrived in 1640 and, after a fierce battle, destroyed almost all of the Portuguese presence. In 1663 the Dutch built the magnificent Fort, with great ramparts and massive bastions, that still stands today and dominates the town.

In 1796 the fort was handed over to the British.

Galle was a major port in Sri Lanka until around 1875, when maritime trade was diverted to Colombo. This well-preserved fort remains a "living" monument with a thriving community within and is one of the eight UNESCO World Heritage Sites found in Sri Lanka.

Galle is also famous for its International Cricket Stadium, where spectators in the grounds and from armchairs around the world have a superb view of the pitch and the magnificent backdrop of the ancient ramparts.

The roads running behind the stadium lead you to the two entrances of the fort, the entrance in to Queen Street being much older. Enclosed within the fort is the old town, with a few hundred houses. You will need a day to wander the 90 acres of streets, or a few hundred rupees and an hour by tuk tuk.

Lying within the fort on Church Street is an amalgamation of buildings constructed by the Dutch, including the Governor's House built in 1683 and the Dutch Military Officers' headquarters built in 1684. In 1848 these buildings became a British Garrison, accommodating soldiers of the 83rd regiment. In 1865 the buildings were combined to create the New Oriental Hotel. The hotel has now been immaculately restored by the prestigious Aman resorts to house the beautiful Amangalla.

The Dutch Groote Kerk (Great Church) was founded in 1640. The present building, dating from 1755, is the oldest Protestant church in Sri Lanka. Opposite the church, the British (replacing the original Dutch structure of 1701), built the belfry and the clock tower. The tolling of the bell signified the death of important citizens.

The Zwart Bastion is probably part of the original Portuguese stronghold and thus the oldest part of the fort.

The British built the lighthouse in 1938 beside the Point Utrecht Bastion, after the original structure which stood beside the Flag Rock Bastion burned down.

In the Arab quarter on Rampart Street is the Meera Mosque, constructed around 1900, possibly on the site of a Portuguese cathedral.

A walk on the ramparts at dusk is inspiring; this romantic stage attracts local lovers for an idyllic rendezvous against the backdrop of a spectacular sunset.

The most wonderful place to stay is the Lighthouse Hotel & Spa, just on the outskirts of Galle. Designed by the famed architect Geoffrey Bawa in Dutch style, this stunning hotel is one of the best in the country and is a member of the small luxury hotels of the world. An experience not to be missed!

Sunset Coast

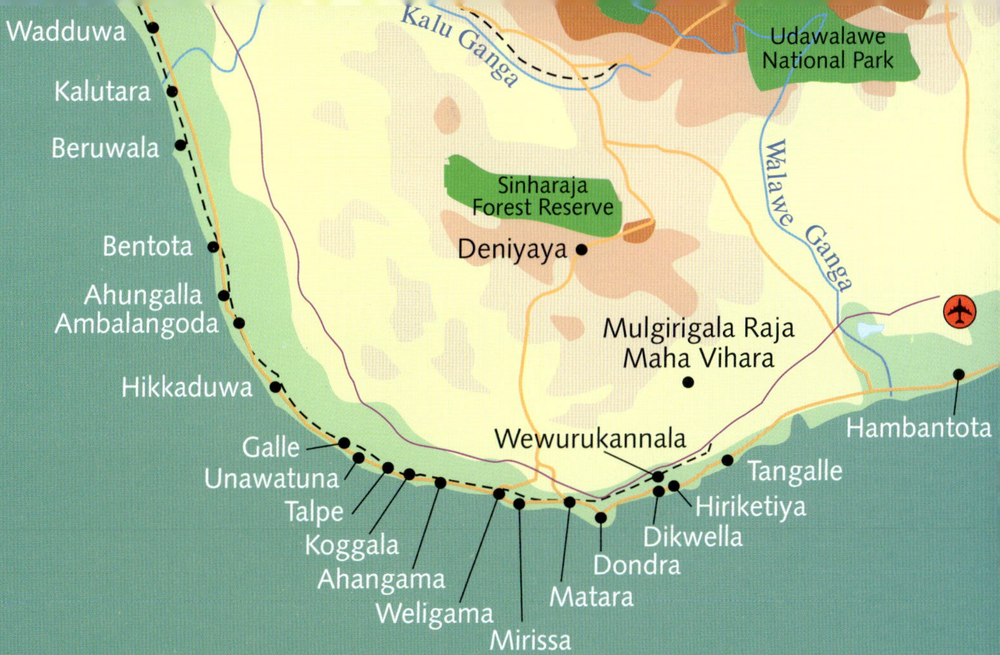

South Coast

දකුණු වෙරළ තීරය

Travelling down Sri Lanka's West Coast you will find mile after mile of beautiful palm fringed golden beaches lining the azure waters of the Indian Ocean.

The main road and train track run parallel to the coast and give delightful glimpses of life in sleepy fishing villages and towns set beside the sea, although nowadays Sri Lanka's Southern Expressway, emerging from the airport near Negombo, will take you at speed up to as far as Hambantota accompanied by stunning inland views.

Generally, the South Coast has a slower pace of life - some towns have resorts and can be busier, while others are far more relaxed and more remote the further you travel. The South has become popular for water sports, especially surfing during the season between December and April, and for yoga retreats with classes all year round. Whilst based on the South Coast you are never far from Sri Lanka's rich culture, incredible wildlife and ancient heritage.

Wherever you decide to trek during your holiday on the island, chances are that you will end your tour on a beach somewhere on the South Coast for some rest and relaxation.

Unawatuna

උනවටුන

N 06° 0' 38"
E 80° 14' 35"

Unawatuna, 3 miles (5 km) from Galle, has a picturesque bay and sandy beach. Suitable for swimming all year round, it has some coral at close proximity to the shore. Snorkelling equipment can be hired on the beachfront, and local hotels can arrange to take you to the shipwrecks offshore. The best views over the bay are from the dagoba on the headland. The Unawatuna Beach is regarded as one of the liveliest and finest beaches in Sri Lanka. With its hip backpacker vibe, this resort is also popular with the locals during weekends and public holidays.

Talpe

තල්පේ

N 05° 59' 43"
E 80° 17' 16"

Further down from Unuwatuna is Talpe Beach, a long unspoilt, quiet and calm stretch of water with a number of activities including snorkelling and kayaking alongside giant turtles. Talpe is a great place to relax and enjoy a superb sunset.

Koggala

කොග්ගල

N 05° 59' 25"
E 80° 19' 21"

Koggala is a small resort with quiet beaches situated at the edge of a lake rich in biodiversity. Visitors can hire boats to ride around the lake exploring some of the islands, where on one island a Buddhist Temple attracts visitors - especially on "Poya" or full moon, and on another, a cinnamon plantation.

Ahangama

අහංගම

N 05° 58' 26"
E 80° 21' 44"

The beaches at Ahangama are famous for their stilt fishermen. Early morning and dusk provide a unique spectacle of men perched on poles intent on the business of catching fish. Stilt positions are sought after and often inherited, passed down from father to son.

Weligama

වැලිගම

N 05° 58′ 30″
E 80° 25′ 36″

The charming bay at Weligama is the beautiful setting for Count de Mauny-Talyande's Taprobane Island. Originally built by the French Count in the 1920's, it has hosted Royalty, aristocracy and eccentrics, giving it a very colourful history. Now privately owned, this tropical island paradise spanning only a couple of acres, with nothing between it and the South Pole, can be rented on a daily basis.

Mirissa

මිරිස්ස

N 05° 56′ 54″
E 80° 28′ 18″

To the south of Weligama is the beautiful village of Mirissa. With lovely beaches, one of the prettiest bays, great waves for surfing and great beachside restaurants, it is a lively town with a bohemian vibe and is a favourite among backpackers.

Mirissa is also renowned for its rich marine life, offering some of the best opportunities to spot turtles close to shore. Most notably, Mirissa is especially famous for dolphin and whale watching during the season from end of November to April. Just half an hour or so from the shore, and your boat will be flanked by hundreds of Spinner Dolphins and with any luck, you will be able to witness the most magical experience of Blue or Sperm Whales emerging majestically from the depths.

Matara

මාතර

N 05° 56′ 37″
E 80° 32′ 36″

Located 7 miles (11 km) from Mirissa, with a population of 40,000, the ancient town of Matara is Sri Lanka's eighth biggest town. This was an important Dutch trading post for elephants and cinnamon, and contains two Dutch forts. Matara Fort was the second most important fort after Galle. The Star Fort, built in 1763, today houses a small museum.

Perched on an island off Matara beach connected by a steel bridge is the stunning Paravi Duwa Buddhist temple from where you will have superb views of the mainland especially at sunset.

Dondra

දෙවුන්දර

N 05° 55′ 10″
E 80° 35′ 19″

Dondra is a small fishing village 3 miles (5 km) from Matara. Meaning "city of the gods", Dondra is Sri Lanka's most southernmost point, 6° from the Equator. On the headland at Dondra Head, stands a magnificent octagonal lighthouse constructed by the British in 1889. If you were to travel directly south across the Indian Ocean from this point, the next landmass you would encounter would be Antarctica.

Elite
GUIDE

Dikwella

දික්වැල්ල

N 05° 58′ 00″
E 80° 41′ 00″

Dikwella is a small costal village 8 miles (13 km) east of Dondra. With its long sandy palm-fringed beach protected by reefs, rocks and sandbars, the Dikwella Beach is ideal for swimming, and Turtle Point offers the perfect spot for snorkelling and swimming with giant turtles close to the shore.

Of the great selection of bars and restaurants available, at the southern end of Dikwella bay is the very trendy Smoke & Bitters, a cocktail bar and smokehouse listed on Asia's 50 Best Bars. With an easy-going vibe, a great selection of cocktails and excellent food created from local produce, it is definitely worth a visit.

Wewurukannala Vihara

වැවුරුකන්නල විහාරය

N 05° 58′ 36″
E 80° 41′ 58″

About 1 mile (1.6 km) inland from Dikwella is Wewurukannala Vihara. The approaching road offers magnificent views of this colossal Buddha statue 164 ft (50 m) high, the tallest on the island. The eight-storey building behind the Buddha contains comic style murals of Buddha's life.

HIRIKETIYA

හිරිකැටිය

N 05° 58′ 00″
E 80° 42′ 00″

Fast becoming a hotspot, a beautiful horseshoe bay surrounded by palm trees and thick tropical jungle with crystal clear water, is the idyllic paradise beach at Hiriketiya. Just over a mile (2 km) from Dikwella, Hiriketiya's picturesque bay, perfect for yoga and meditation, is gaining significant attention, especially among surfers in peak season and digital nomads working remotely enjoying the bohemian vibe.

TANGALLE

තංගල්ල

N 06° 01′ 00″
E 80° 47′ 00″

Located about 9 miles (15 km) from Hiriketiya, Tangalle is a low-key resort with simple guesthouses along with a handful of villas and hotels. It boasts a pristine stretch of coastline, with coves, golden sand beaches lined with swaying palm trees, and turquoise blue waters ideal for surfers, especially beginners. This serves as the perfect base for exploring nearby attractions through daily excursions.

Despite its growing popularity this small fishing village has managed to retain its traditional beauty and charm.

N 06° 07' 23"
E 80° 44' 11"

මුල්ගිරිගල රජ මහා විහාරය

MULGIRIGALA RAJA MAHA VIHARA

Situated in the southern Hambantota district, rising 673 ft (205 m) from the forest, is the Rock of Mulgirigala. The ancient temple built here consists of a series of terraces with shrines cut into the rock housing murals and Buddha images. The Bo Tree on the upper terrace is considered be a shoot from one of the 32 saplings of Anuradhapura's Sri Maha Bodhi planted during the reign of King Devanampiya Tissa (250-210 BC). According to ancient chronicles, the Mulgirigala Vihara was constructed by King Saddhatissa (137-119 BC) who built a stupa on the summit enshrining relics of the Buddha.

The monastery housed a collection of Pali manuscripts which was one of the most valuable libraries on the island. It was from this collection that in 1827, a transcript of the tika (commentary), on the Mahavamsa (Great Chronicle), was discovered by a British archaeologist which was used for its translation, detailing a unique historical record of the Island beginning with the arrival of Indo Aryans in 483 BC to the 4th century AD.

The temple also possessed all the commentaries of entire Tripitaka (Pali Cannon) on Ola leaves in Sinhala script.

UDAWALAWE NATIONAL PARK

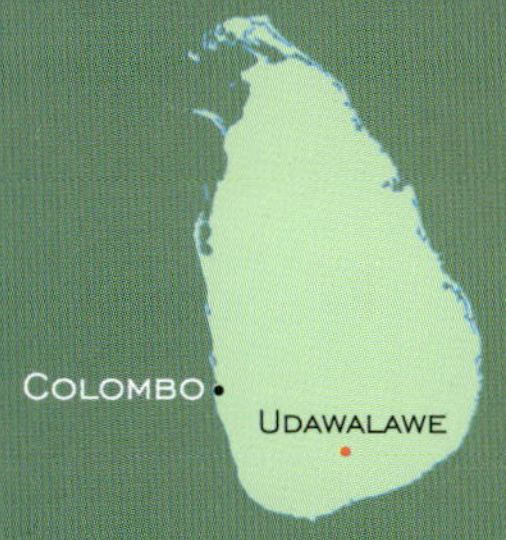

උඩවලවේ ජාතික වනෝද්‍යානය

N 06° 26′ 18″
E 80° 53′ 18″

Around 40 miles (65 km) north of Tangalle lies the Udawalawe National Park. This picturesque park of scrub jungle, wetlands and grasslands centred around the Udawalawe reservoir, is home to a variety of animals including the water buffalo, monkeys, crocodiles, sloth bear, and the occasional leopard. The surrounding marsh and wetlands attract an abundance of both endemic and migratory birds. The park's star attraction is the Asian elephant which can be seen throughout the year.

A typical safari includes a jeep and a local guide who is knowledgeable about the park's wildlife and the best spotting locations; the optimal viewing times are at dawn or dusk when the animals are most active.

HAMBANTOTA

හම්බන්තොට

N 06° 07' 33"
E 81° 07' 32"

The largest town on the southeastern coast is Hambantota, a small fishing village in the dry zone. It has a large Muslim population of mainly Malay descent, whose ancestors would have arrived in sampans from Indonesia during the Dutch occupation. This is the centre for the production of salt by the age-old method of evaporating seawater from shallow saltpans.

Being in close proximity to the wildlife sanctuaries, Hambantota can be used as a base to visit Bundala Sanctuary and Wirawila-Tissa Bird Sanctuary or as a stop on the way to Yala Wildlife Sanctuary. This area is also renowned for its superb curd made from buffalo milk. You can't miss the hanging pots on stalls along the roadside.

Bundala National Park

Colombo

Bundala

N 06° 12' 50"
E 81° 13' 30"

බූන්දල

Covering an area of 15,300 acres (6,200 hectares) along the coast, Bundala National Park is much smaller than Yala and has the reputation of being a bird sanctuary.

Around 150 species of bird can be found here, including peacocks, storks, spoonbills, ibis, pelicans, flamingos, egrets and migrant birds such as plovers and sandpipers.

Jeeps can be hired locally and a tracker will join you at the entrance to the park. The sanctuary consists of a series of shallow lagoons surrounded by quite thick scrubland. This makes elephant spotting more difficult, but it is a good place for observing crocodiles. Other animals roaming this sanctuary are monkeys, jackals, rabbits, snakes, spotted deer, wild boar, porcupines, pangolins and civet cats.

N 08° 33' 10"
E 81° 14' 17"

TRINCOMALEE

ත්‍රිකුණාමලය

Trincomalee has one of the world's finest natural harbours. It is the fifth largest in the world, covering an area of 55 sq miles (142 sq km). Operating from ancient times it may have been the place where Prince Mahinda first landed in the 3rd century BC on his way to Mihintale.

In the modern era, this highly strategic port, first sighted by the Dutch around 1617 on a brief reconnaissance visit, was taken over by the Portuguese in 1624. From 1639, it then changed hands between the Dutch, the King of Kandy, the Dutch, the French, the British, the French, the Dutch and finally in 1795 the British – their first possession in Ceylon.

Natural Harbour

Admiral Lord Horatio Nelson visited Trincomalee in 1775 as midshipman onboard HMS Seahorse, and is quoted as saying it was "the finest harbour in the world".

During World War II, "Trinco" became the headquarters of the combined Allied fleets in South Asia. On April 8th 1942, the Japanese carried out an air attack on the harbour; however, having been alerted, the Allied forces had sent the fleet to sea and only two ships were destroyed by the Japanese.

Fort Frederick, located on a promontory to the east of the town, was originally built by the Portuguese in 1624, and was named in honour of Frederick, Duke of York by the British in 1803.

Wellington House was named after the Duke of Wellington who, after a bout of malaria, convalesced in this house, missing the ship that was to carry him to Egypt. This ship sank in the Gulf of Aden losing all on board, so the Duke had a lucky escape and was thus saved for his historic encounter with Napoleon at Waterloo.

The road that bisects the fort leads to the Swami Rock and the Koneswaram Kovil dedicated to Shiva, which stands where the Temple of a Thousand Columns existed hundreds of years before Christ. That temple was destroyed by the Portuguese, who used the stonework to build their fort.

Immediately Behind the Temple is Lover's Leap, so called after the reputed suicide of a Dutch official's daughter, throwing herself off the rock as her lover sailed away abandoning her. However, there is evidence that she did no such thing, marrying eight years later.

Travelling 5 miles (8 km) north-west of Trincomalee, a turning off the Trincomalee-Anuradhapura road leads to the Hot Springs at Kanniya. Here there are seven hot water wells of varying temperature said to have mystical therapeutic and healing properties.

Nilaveli is a small village 7 miles (11 km) north of Trincomalee, where the beaches are superb, with soft white sand and calm seas during April to October season when rainfall is much lower than in the southwest.

The best place to stay in Nilaveli is the Pigeon Island Beach Resort situated on a beautiful stretch of secluded beach. The rooms are luxurious and the hotel provides without doubt the best food in town. A few hundred metres offshore lies Pigeon Island, a great place for snorkelling around the colourful coral reefs, diving and fishing. The hotel can provide a motorboat for trips to the island and also organise exciting excursions for dolphin and whale watching not far from the shore.

Pigeon Island

GIRIHANDU SEYA, THIRIYAYA

ගිරිහඬු සේයා

Around 20 miles (32 km) north of Nilaveli located in Thiriyaya is the Girihandu Seya temple. What is unique about this temple is that it is said to be the site of the oldest edifice dedicated to Buddhism.

Legend has it that during the lifetime of the Buddha two merchant brothers Thapassu and Balluka came to the island of Lanka. The Buddha had given them a lock of His hair, which they had placed in a golden casket and carried with them to venerate on their travels.

The two brothers spent the night on a hilltop where they placed the golden casket on a rock and covered it with a white cloth. The next morning the merchants were stunned to find the casket embedded in the rock and therefore decided to build a cairn enshrining the casket containing the Hair relic of the Buddha. A Dagoba was later built over the site and during the reign of King Aggabodhi (VI) (733-772) the Vatadage was commissioned. Vatadages are very rare and consists of a central Dagoba with four seated Buddha statues facing the cardinal points encircled with concentric stone pillars that once would have supported a conical roof.

Batticaloa

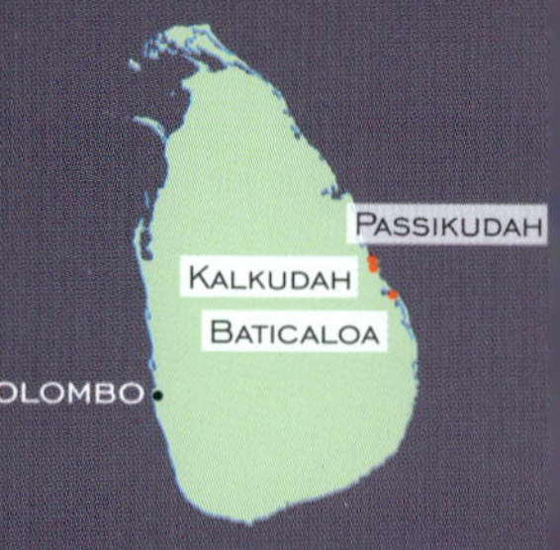

N 07° 43' 04"
E 81° 42' 41"

Located on the eastern coast, Batticaloa is a town surrounded by a lagoon steeped in colonial heritage from the advent of Portuguese, the Dutch, to the British.

As well as three lagoons, there are colourful Hindu Kovils, a lighthouse, and the remains of the Dutch Fort. Kallady Beach is superb for a swim and getting away from it all, perhaps enjoying an amazing sunrise or watching the local fisherfolk bringing in the night's haul. Batticaloa is famously known for its 'singing fish'. Close to the Kallady Bridge, between April and September around the full-moon at dusk, a unique high pitch sound emanates from the depths of the water. Locals claim that this is the singing fish living in the lagoon.

About 20 miles (32 km) north of Batticaloa, at Passikudah and Kalkudah, are two pristine soft golden sandy bays with shallow, calm, azure waters. These idyllic beaches are considered to be among the finest in the country.

Elite
GUIDE

Point Break

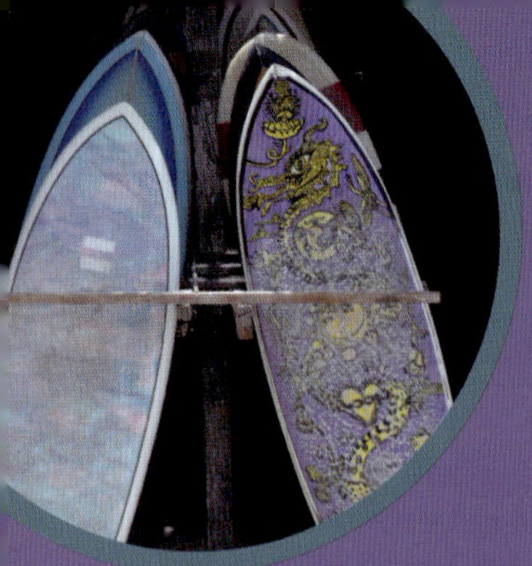

N 06° 50' 25"
E 81° 50' 12"

ARUGAM BAY

ආරුගම් බොක්ක

Arugam Bay, situated on the east coast, is recognised as one of the best surfing sites in the world. It is said to be in the global top ten for surfing, and periodically hosts international competitions where surfers from all over the world come to compete. Its busiest season with world-famous waves, runs from May until October.

Surfers first came to Arugam Bay, then a little jungle fishing village with a few shacks on the beach, in the 1980's. The warm tropical waters lining long deserted unspoilt beaches, with isolated bays set alongside crocodile filled lagoons, rapidly turned into a hot spot for surfing. The town then grew around surfing culture with a hippie vibe, attracting those seeking a bohemian lifestyle.

Of the many surfing points found in Arugam Bay, Whiskey Point north of Arugam Bay is a favourite for beginners and intermediates, the size of waves ranging from 2 to 6 ft (0.6 - 1.8 m). Here the rocks provide a great viewpoint and, in the evening, the whole area transforms into a party atmosphere.

South of Arugam Bay other amazing surf spots include Crocodile Rock and Elephant Rock, both of which are a must-visit location for surfers.

කුමණ ජාතික
වනෝද්‍යානය

N 06° 30' 47"
E 81° 41' 16"

KUMANA NATIONAL PARK

Around 12 miles (20 km) south of Arugam Bay is Kumana National Park covering over 88,000 acres (35,600 hectares) and established in 1938. With over 255 species, this is one of the most important nesting and breeding grounds for birds. Thousands of birds migrate to the Kumana Villu a massive 494 acre (200 hectare) natural mangrove swamp as well as the many tanks and lagoons to nest and breed every year between months of April to July.

The park is famed for its large flocks of migratory Waterfowl and Water birds, other species include Eurasian spoonbills, Black-necked stork, Lesser adjunt, Pintail snipes, Glossy ibis and Purple heron. Rare visitors include the Yellow-footed green pigeon, Malabar trogon and Red-faced malkoha.

Other animals found in Kumana include the Sri Lankan Elephant, Leopard, Fishing cat, Wild boar and Golden Jackal, the Mugger Crocodile and Indian black turtle.

Elite
GUIDE

කුඩුම්බිගල පිරිවෙන

COLOMBO

KUDUMBIGAL

KUDUMBIGALA MONASTERY

N 06° 40' 21"
E 81° 44' 35"

Inside of Kumana National Park is the beautiful forest hermitage of Kudumbigala. The hundreds of caves here were inhabited by Buddhist monks from the 1st century BC and in some caves ancient Brahmi script is still visible.

The forest path takes you past a new stupa, and other monastic remains scattered over the rocky hilltop up to the caves. Further on, a granite hill with ancient steps cut into it leads to the summit with an unusually shaped brick stupa and superb panoramic views.

Cave Monastery

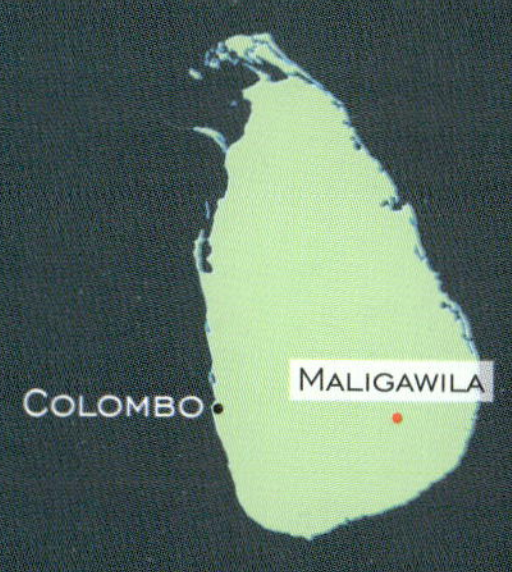

N 06° 43' 08"
E 81° 21' 10"

Maligawila Raja Maha Vihara

මාලිගාවිල රජ මහා විහාරය

Discovered in 1951 in the jungles close to the village of Maligawila, broken into many pieces, was one of the best examples of an ancient Buddha.

Carved out of a limestone rock during the 7th century, the Maligawila Buddha statue is the tallest free-standing Buddha statue on the island. After restoration in the 1980s, this beautiful image rises to a height of 37 ft (11 m) and is styled similarly to the Aukana Buddha located south of Mihintale, built in the 5th century.

KATARAGAMA

කතරගම

N 06° 25' 08"
E 81° 19' 59"

About 10 miles (16 km) north of Tissamaharama is Kataragama, a sacred place for Buddhists, Hindus, Muslims and Christians.

This small town is not often visited by tourists, but is a regular pilgrimage site for the islanders throughout the year. As a holy site, it ranks on the same level of reverence as Adam's Peak, but is slightly easier to get to!

Rituals

In the 2nd century BC, King Dutugamunu (161-137 BC) built the Maha Devale shrine dedicated to Skanda, the Hindu God of war, known as the "Kataragama Deviyo" after he successfully overthrew the ruler Elara in Anuradhapura. This shrine is said to contain the lance of this twelve-armed Hindu god.

Beyond the Hindu shrine is the Kiri Vihara, a dagoba dating from the 1st century BC. There are also smaller shrines to Vishnu, Ganesh and Pattini.

Sri Lankans from all over the island visit Kataragama; it is more of a Sri Lankan custom than a religious one. Individuals, families and minibus loads make the trip once a year or sometimes more. Vows are undertaken and carried out here and offerings are made to the deities, seeking blessings for themselves or others and to give thanks for past blessings.

The Esala full moon festival (July/August) draws many thousands of people to Kataragama, when some entranced devotees carry out ritualistic vows, such as being hung on hooks that are pierced in their backs and having skewers put through their cheeks and tongue. They are then swung in procession around the holy site.

Fire walking is part of the festival purification ritual, as devotees seek blessings from the goddess Pattini.

යාල ජාතික වනෝද්‍යානය
யால தேசிய வனம்
YALA NATIONAL PARK

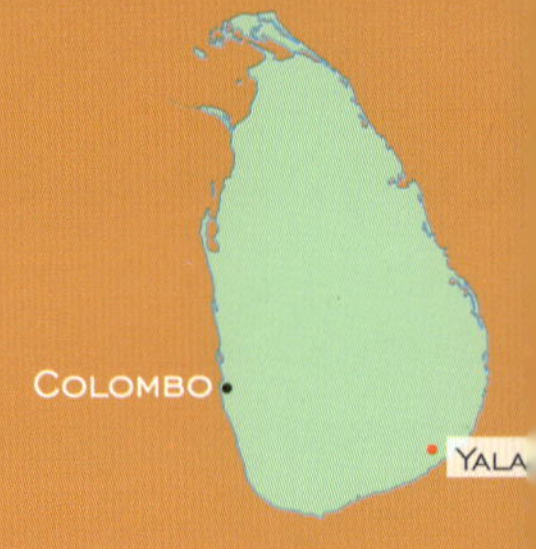

N 06° 27' 38"
E 81° 28' 16"

යාල ජාතික වනෝද්‍යානය

YALA NATIONAL PARK

Covering an area of 500 sq miles (1300 sq km), Yala National Park is the biggest and most visited wildlife sanctuary in Sri Lanka, ideal for viewing the island's natural treasures.

With a diversity of habitats, including dense jungle, plains, streams, lagoons and rocky outcrops, the terrain is extremely suitable for Sri Lanka's leopard, Yala's star attraction.

Jungles

Other animals found in Yala include elephant, sloth bear, crocodile, monkey, buffalo, wild boar, deer, land and water monitor, mongoose and jackal. Nocturnal animals include Indian civets, pangolin, porcupine and slender loris. There are 150 different species of birds including painted stork, the rare black-necked stork, green bee-eater, pompadour green pigeon, imperial green pigeon and the orange-breasted green pigeon. Two endemic birds are the Sri Lankan jungle fowl and the brown-capped babbler. Migrants include the common blue-tailed bee-eater, the Brahminy Myrna and the rosy starling.

The best time to see Yala's wildlife is either at dawn or dusk. Safaris start at 6am and at 3pm.

Other wildlife reserves include Wilpattu National Park in the North Western Province, Udawalawe in the Southern Province and Minneriya National Park in the North Central Province. Every year the largest concentration of Asian Elephants takes place on the receding shores of the Minneriya Lake. "The Gathering" in Minneriya is one of the most fantastic events in the international wildlife calendar peaking in August and September when over 300 hundred elephants congregate.

Elite
GUIDE

Elite
GUIDE

tuktuk
rental.com
WHATSAPP
OK NOW TO DRIVE YOUR OWN TUKTUK!

USEFUL VOCABULARY

'Ayubowan'
Sri Lankan greeting which means
'May you be blessed with long life'

ENGLISH	SINHALA	TAMIL
Hello	Ayubowan	Vanakkam
Please	Karunakara	Thayavuyseidu
Thank you	Isthuthi	Nandri
Yes	Ow	Ohm
No	Naha	Illay
I	Mama	Naan
We	Api	Naangal
You	Oba	Neengal
Friend	Yaluwa	Nanbar
Name	Nama	Peyar
Come	Enna	Vaarungal
Go	Yanna	Poengal
Book	Potha	Putthagam
Look	Balanna	Paarungal
Like	Kamathi	Viruppam
Where?	Koheda	Engay
What?	Mokadda	Enna
When?	Kavadda	Eppa
This	Meka	Idhu
That	Araka	Adhu
Mother	Amma	Ammaa
Father	Thatha	Appaa
Elder Sister	Akka	Akkaa
Elder Brother	Aiya	Annaa
Younger Sister	Nangi	Thangai/Thangachchi
Younger Brother	Malli	Thambi
Boy	Kolla	Aan pillai
Girl	Kella	Pen pillai
English	Ingirisi	Aangkilam
Bank	Bankuwa	Vangi
Doctor	Dosthara	Vaiththiyar
Shop	Sappuwa	Kadai
Drink	Beema	Paanam
Eat	Kanna	Saappidungal
Sleep	Nindha	Nitthirai
Bread	Paan	Paan
Water	Wathura	Thanneer
Coffee	Kopi	Koeppi
Tea	The	Theayneer
Milk	Kiri	Paal
Vegetable	Elolu	Marakkari
Coconut	Pol	Thengaai
Mango	Amba	Maampazham
Delicious	Rasai	Rusi
Morning	Ude	Kaalai
Afternoon	Dawal	Pahal
Evening	Havasa	Maalai
Night	Rae	Iravu
Today	Ada	Indru
Tomorrow	Heta	Naalai
Yesterday	Eeya	Netru
Week	Sumanaya	Vaaram
Month	Maseya	Maasam / Maadham
Day	Davasa	Thinam
Year	Aurudda	Varusham
Hat	Thoppiya	Thoppi
Shoes	Sapaththu	Kaalani/Chappaaththu
Sarong	Sarama	Saaram
Soap	Saban	Saukaaram
Bathroom	Nanakamare	Kuliyal arai
Hospital	Ispiritaale	Vaithiya saalai
0	Binduwa	Saivar
1	Eka	Ondru
2	Deka	Irandu
3	Thuna	Moondru
4	Hathara	Naangu
5	Paha	Aindhu
6	Haya	Aaru
7	Hatha	Eazhu
8	Ata	Ettu
9	Namaya	Onpadhu
10	Dahaya	Paththu
20	Wissa	Iruppadhu
30	Thiha	Muppadhu
40	Hathaliya	Naappadhu
50	Panaha	Aimppadhu
100	Seeya	Nooru
500	Pan Seeya	Ainooru
1000	Daaha	Aayiram
10000	Daaha Dahaya	Paththaayiram
100000	Laksaya	Noorayiram

English	Sinhala	Tamil
How are you?	Kohomada?	Eppadi irukkureengal?
I'm fine	Mama hondhai	Naan nallaai irukkiren
What is the time?	Velaava Keeyada?	Mani eth-tanai?
What is your name?	Nama mokadda?	Ungal peyar enna?
My name is...	Mage nama...	En peyar...
How much is this?	Meka kiyada?	Idhu evalavu?

Sri Lanka Tourism
80 Galle Road
Colombo 3
Tel +94 11 242 6900
info@srilanka.travel
www.srilanka.travel

Sri Lanka

YOU'LL COME BACK FOR MORE

Contact details

24 Hr Contact Center	**+94117771979**
General	**+94197335555**
Ticket Office	**+94197335555**
Customer Affairs	**+94197331627**
SriLankan Cargo	**+94197333280**
SriLankan Holidays	**+94197333838**
FlySmiLes	**+94197333333**

SriLankan Airlines Ltd
Airline Centre
Bandaranaike International Airport
Katunayake
Sri Lanka

General Website:	**www.srilankan.com**
SriLankan Holidays:	**www.srilankanholidays.com**
General:	**reservations@srilankan.com**
SriLankan Cargo:	**https://ww.srilankancargo.com**
FlySmiLes:	**https://www.srilankan.com/flysmiles**